Illusions of *Opportunity*

The American Dream in Question

John E. Schwarz

W. W. Norton & Company

New York London

For information about permission to reproduce selections from this book,
write to Permissions, W. W. Norton & Company, Inc., 500 Fifth Avenue,
New York, NY 10110.

The text of this book is composed in 10.75/15 pt Adobe Caslon with the
display set in Franklin Gothic.
Book manufacturing by The Maple-Vail Book Manufacturing
Book design by BTD.

LIBRARY OF CONGRESS CATALOGING-IN-PUBLICATION DATA

Schwarz, John E.
    Illusions of opportunity : the American dream in question / John E.
Schwarz.
        p. cm.
    Includes bibliographical references and index.
    ISBN 0-393-04534-X
    1. Work ethic—United States. 2. United States—Moral conditions. 3.
Labor policy—United States. 4. Labor market—United States. 5. United
States—Social policy.
HD8072.5.S83 1997
306'.0973—dc21   97-2282
                                                          CIP

W. W. Norton & Company, Inc., 500 Fifth Avenue, New York, NY 10110
http://www.wwnorton.com
W. W. Norton & Company Ltd., 10 Coptic Street, London WC1A 1PU

1 2 3 4 5 6 7 8 9 0

For my teachers

CONTENTS

For some time I've been troubled by the fact that a number of families I've met who work hard cannot seem to support themselves adequately despite trying to find better paying work. I wrote this book with the story in mind of the Bartelles, a family whom I interviewed at considerable length. Ernst Bartelle was 57 years old at the time of our interview. I got to know him as an intellegent, honest, and responsible person who had worked full-time his whole life. To my mind he was a person of remarkable integrity. He was a maintenance worker at a school a few miles from his home in Denver. He and his family, consisting of his wife, Anna, and two teenage children, had so little money that sometimes they went for days eating only potatoes or potatoes and eggs in order to get by. Anna, who had a full-time clerical job, said to me, "You ever seen a hamster in a cage? It just runs and runs on its wheel and gets nowhere. That's what I feel like sometimes." Ernst had tried unsuccessfully to get other jobs. Believing in America as a land of opportunity, Ernst took responsibility for his and his family's condition. Although he had earned a high-school degree at a time when that was deemed sufficient qualification for success and when many of his peers had not, he believed that he could have done something differently. Assuming the blame, he saw himself as a failure, as worthless. In considerable pain, he had even considered suicide.

I interviewed a number of families facing hard times that, like the Bartelles, accepted personal responsibility. Still others I interviewed, by contrast, had very different explanations for their misfortune. Some blamed a system that they thought helped the rich and hurt the poor, or they blamed the economy; others blamed a spouse or a boss; a few blamed the government; and some believed that their experiences were the product of plain bad luck. Whatever their reaction or explanation, whether they blamed themselves or others, the essentials of their experiences were similar: responsible behavior and a lot of hard work over many years had led nowhere. These families had not been able to control their lives in a manner that they believed to be adequate. Without exception, the experiences had left them distraught.

I wrote this book in the belief—and the hope—that it matters to Americans whether or not their nation lives up to the ethos to which it subscribes. The ethos voices the fundamental belief of Americans in the power and the capacity of the individual. It expresses the American idea that the opportunity exists in this abundant land for individuals of strong character who are willing to work hard and persevere to get ahead and find a measure of success. By dint of their own efforts, given the opportunity that exists in America, all Americans can make a decent living and take care of themselves, the ethos says. All Americans can be independent. I believe that whether the nation lives up to this ethos matters morally in terms of right and wrong and substantively in terms of the spirit and quality of life that both the nation and its people enjoy. The Bartelles' story raises questions about the validity of the American ethos, questions to which we cannot be indifferent.

Many readers, I imagine, will feel some sympathy at hearing the stories of the Bartelles and the others. The question that needs to be answered, however, is who bears responsibility for the Bartelles' situation. What is particularly important for the nation to determine is whether the experiences of families like the Bartelles are reasonably within their own control and thus are primarily their responsibility, or whether the outcomes are essentially beyond their personal control. Were only a handful of families to have these experiences, perhaps there would be little reason for our interest. However, the possibility exists that these stories describe the circumstances of millions of families. How we ultimately view the moral and substantive success of America, how we see our obligations toward our fellow Americans, and how we interpret the economic and social problems facing the nation hinge on how commonplace the Bartelles' story is and whether American families do in fact have a reasonable level of control over their own destinies.

The evidence seems compelling that ample opportunity exists for anyone who wants it and is willing to put in the effort. During the past three decades, the American economy has grown at a speed near the growth rate that England experienced during the zenith of the Industrial Revolution. It has generated literally tens of millions of new jobs in those thirty years. It seems that no economy growing this fast could lack decent opportunities for people willing to take advantage of them. Yet

I cannot dismiss the Bartelles and their story, and similar stories of other hardworking and caring families.

The evidence presented in this book is in part based on first-ever measurements of the availability of decent-paying jobs nationally. Set within the context of elemental principles fundamental to the nation ever since its birth, the discussion will show that the number of Americans closed out of minimally adequate opportunity surpasses the total populations of the one hundred largest American cities combined. The number left out amounts to nearly four times the population of the entire metropolitan area of New York City. This sizable shortage of opportunity for American families is not new but has existed now for more than three decades. It carries enormous implications for a wide range of national problems. Until the nation squarely faces the reality of the scarcity of opportunity raised in these pages, it will be unable to attain a lasting rebirth.*

To confront these issues, the nation must find the path to reconcile two powerful world views. The first of these accents the idea of the free market, the second emphasizes the idea of the equal moral worth of human beings. These two ideas are often seen to be the same, yet they are not. The importance of the distinction between the two, and its consequences for clarifying the choices facing the nation, will become clear as the discussion unfolds.

What the nation needs is leadership with the vision to identify the problems we face candidly and the courage to create and promote honest solutions. To fail to act represents no less than a national repudiation of the American Dream, a denunciation of the very soul of the nation.

*Issues about statistics on inflation have arisen recently that cast doubt on previous calculations of the worth of workers' wages after inflation. Such issues do not affect the conclusions of this book, however, as Appendix C shows.

ILLUSIONS OF OPPORTUNITY

Chapter **1**

THE PROBLEM

Disquieting doubts have crept into America's consciousness over the past thirty years. Mounting social pathologies, troubling economic uncertainties, and rising political disillusion have left many feeling that something is wrong, that the nation's bright lustre has become tarnished, that the nation has somehow lost its way. To ascertain the root of our fears, recover our moral bearings, and renew the nation's sense of purpose, we must begin at the beginning: with our fundamental principles, with our basic creed. In Abraham Lincoln's words, America is dedicated to a proposition.

The nation's creed asserts the moral equality of all. Belief in it connects each of us to the whole and thus to one another. It gives us a sense of shared fate, despite the centrifugal forces of our many ethnic, racial, and religious differences, and the great importance we attach to individuality. The glue that binds an immensely diverse people cannot be a common blood or unifying religion, but must instead be a shared idea, a secular religion (from the Latin for "tying together") that supplies us with a common sense of our responsibilities to one another. George Will thus rightly describes us as a creedal, not a tribal, nation.[1] And as Francis Fukuyama points out in *The End of History and the Last Man*, communities that share a language or creed based on good and evil will be far more enduring than those based simply on self-interest. In effect, the message of our creed, what it requires of us, and the place it holds in our tradition are tantamount to describing the genetic and familial ties that the English have with one another, or the French, or the Germans.[2] Out of our enormous array of differences, it is what makes us one people.

A central component of this creed is called the American Ethos, or the American Dream. Every American today instinctively knows the ethos: that every individual should be able to get ahead and gain some measure of success through actions and means that are under his or her own control.[3] Roger Angell describes it as the faith that we all belong somewhere within a rational and forgiving system that in the end rewards hard work, intelligence, and sacrifice.[4] The ethos is that everyone who steadfastly practices certain practical virtues will find a place at the table. No one need be left out, unless he or she voluntarily chooses to be. These virtues—self-control, discipline, effort, perseverance, and responsibility—stand at the core of our sense of morality and our idea of good character, and are essential to the success and safety of a good society. To fail to reward them would be to diminish and devalue them as virtues. No value survives forever on incantations alone.

That America should be a land of opportunity where every hardworking person who perseveres can find a respected place is an idea whose roots run so deep in American history that it dates back to the Declaration of Independence and the very founding of the Republic. So universally is it accepted among Americans as a moral foundation that it transcends politics and political party identification—Democrat, Republican, libertarian, religious right, Perotista, independent—of voters and nonvoters alike, no matter their age, gender, race, or ethnic background. It is what unites us in the present and, in turn, unites the present with the past.

The ethos also sets forth a standard of justice that holds each individual accountable, for it assumes that one's fate is in large measure under one's own control. With this belief in mind, Congress named its landmark welfare reform bill of 1996 "the Personal Responsibility Act." Yet as James Madison pointed out in the *Federalist* No. 63, "Responsibility, in order to be reasonable, must be limited to objects within the power of the responsible party."[5] A community in which individuals lack control over their own fate loses the moral right to apply an authentic notion of personal accountability.

To many Americans, the very idea of being wholly human dissolves if we have little or no control over our own fate. If it is true that absolute power corrupts, so can absolute powerlessness. The ability to exercise a reasonable level of control over one's own future is essential, in the American way of thinking, not simply due to the virtues it will affirm or the sense of justice it permits but because it defines our idea of fully realized humanity itself.

As a result, the notion that people do have a capacity to control their own destinies is an enormously strong, almost insistent feature of our American culture. The stories of penni-less immigrants who came to these shores and became success-ful are as legion as they are inspiring, fostering a belief that anyone can start anew in this country and succeed. Principal Joe Clark tells his students at Eastside High School in Patterson, New Jersey: "Don't you know, no one can hold you down unless you consent to it."[5] Madeline Cartwright, principal of James G. Blaine Public School in North Philadelphia, challenges her stu-dents: "I'm telling you, there's things you can do."[7] America is a land, in the fashion of Horatio Alger, Jr., where "God helps those who help themselves."

Nonetheless, many people believe that over the past three decades a dangerous anti-ethos has arisen: the idea that the indi-vidual American is not responsible for his or her own fate. From the point of view of these observers, too many individuals have come to see themselves as victims rather than as agents, to feel sorry for themselves instead of working to pick themselves up—a mentality that government assistance programs helped to spawn and now continue to reinforce. With the expansion of government has come a feeling of entitlement and an emphasis on rights over responsibilities. The creed of personal account-ability so important to the American ethos has withered, and with that has come a rise in welfare, illegitimacy, crime, and other social pathologies—the price the society has paid for the abandonment of character. In the end, William Bennett reminds us, "the state of the union depends on the character of its citi-zens."[8]

Or has something gone wrong with the ethos itself? The premise that individuals can control and so be personally respon-sible for their own lives presumes that the opportunity to do so exists. Generations of Americans have called this "the land of opportunity." But is it, still? Does opportunity remain available and adequate to the needs of the American people, sufficient to enable them to take control of their own lives? Does this ethos, which is expected to connect us and provide the moral underpinnings of a just and healthy society, reflect the reality that American families actually experience in their everyday lives? Are the problems troubling society today due to the disintegration of values and character, or to a genuine lack of opportunity that prevents individuals and families from being able to determine their own futures?

The answers we are offered rely on little more than intuitive sense and anecdotal information. Some say good jobs are there for the asking, all a worker needs to do is to look in the daily newspapers;[9] others tell of employers who have so many applications on file for jobs that they can easily keep wages low and, if necessary, rid themselves of workers.[10] One scholar says that the very brief time individuals stay unemployed before finding a new job stands as compelling testimony to the availability of opportunity;[11] yet a news story reports that 1,000 people lined up and waited for hours to apply for a handful of temporary jobs with no benefits at a General Motors plant.[12] The chairman of Pacific Telesis informs us that over half of the 6,400 workers applying for 700 operator jobs at $7 per hour with his company were not qualified and could not read at the seventh-grade level. But 2,700 applicants *were* qualified for the 700 jobs.[13] One person points to the welfare queen who cheats the taxpayer, and a series of private-sector programs that have gotten good jobs for welfare recipients who are willing to work. Another tells the story of a welfare recipient who tries and perseveres but has gotten nowhere.

These contradictory narratives, each resulting from a cobbling together of bits and pieces of evidence, have become central to our politics. Each side routinely exploits its narrative for political gain. The debate doesn't move us forward, however. Instead, it polarizes and ultimately shackles us.

The struggle between left and right infusing our politics, played out particularly in our social and economic policies, isn't mainly a battle between different world views of morality or the good society. It is, in part, of course. Looking beneath the surface, however, it is even more a conflict about the degree to which a society that every side perceives as essentially good—a society that provides enough opportunity for all—actually exists. Each side of the political debate fundamentally agrees that the deserving should be helped, and that those who try and cannot help themselves *are* the deserving. The American ethos is common currency; in the end, all sides concur that there are certain entitlements, and that foremost among them is the right to opportunity.

What, then, does economic opportunity mean according to the lights of American thinking? To what extent does opportunity commensurate with American standards exist in the nation, both now and in the recent past? What implications do the answers to these questions have for an understanding of the troubles presently facing the nation? What do the answers teach us about our policies now—and what they must become in the future—with respect to job creation, welfare, child support, health care measures, minimum wage laws, education, job training, and labor organization, among others? What are the implications in terms of the role government should play in the economy, and in terms of what it means to say that the economy is a success or a failure? Do today's measures of the economy accurately inform us or fundamentally mislead us? If there isn't enough opportunity, why not? What lessons are there for nations around the world that are looking to the American example?

This book is about the answers to these and other related questions—answers that will likely surprise both the right and the left.

Chapter 2

VOICES OF THE
FOUNDERS

■ deas of the present often have their origins in the past, and so it is with our ideas about opportunity. They date back to the nation's birth and before. On June 12, 1776, the Virginia convention adopted the first Bill of Rights in America. Composed by George Mason, its initial provision declared that "all men are by nature equally free and independent." Soon thereafter Thomas Jefferson completed his draft of the Declaration of Independence, requested of him by the Continental Congress. It boldly proclaimed, "We hold these truths to be sacred and undeniable; that all men are created equal and independant."[1]

These words affirmed not only a transcendent political principle but also a visionary proposition having to do with economic opportunity. To the contemporary ear, words like "independent" and "equal" convey mostly a political and not an economic meaning. But that was not the case for the founders of the country, for whom the term "independence" encapsulated an entire doctrine of political *economy* that they considered necessary to support a nation capable of nurturing and sustaining a free, stable, and moral republic. Grasping the founders' beliefs about ideas such as independence is crucial not merely in order to appreciate their most basic views about what constitutes a well-ordered nation but also in order to comprehend our own ideas, such as the American Dream, that are central to defining what we consider a decent society today.

The American revolutionaries' beliefs about independence had deep roots. The language of "moral economy," inherited from seventeenth-century English working people, held that there ought to be a sphere of economic life delivering a customary standard of living with a basic level of dignity, what was sometimes called a "comfortable subsistence," that households could earn on their own and manage as they saw fit. This sphere of economic control by individual households was called "competency." Competency implied that individual households had a right to access to the means of production necessary to attain a minimally dignified living standard,[2] a condition that was crucial to a successful society in the minds of men such as James Madison. For the future of the new world, he observed, "the best distribution (of occupations) is that which most favor . . . competency in the greatest number of citizens."[3]

The idea of independence, to the founders, presumed competency.[4] Independence had to do with whether an individual was or was not subject to the control of anyone else, economically or politically. To be independent, a household needed to own sufficient property, or have other means, permitting it to produce an acceptable standard of living without having to become indebted to or dependent upon the will of anyone else.

This understanding of independence as ownership of economic means capable of delivering a minimally dignified standard of living was as familiar to the everyday farmer, artisan, and journeyman in America as it was to the Revolutionary leaders, and just as fundamental to all of them.[5]

The word "free," in turn, contained an economic dimension that was tied to the idea of independence.[6] A "free man," or "free citizen," was "one who was independent of others for life's sustenance,"[7] free to act "as [he thinks] fit . . . without asking leave, or depending upon the Will of any other Man," to use the words of John Locke.[8] "Freedom," Thomas Paine said, "is destroyed by dependence."[9] A person who was not independent could not be said to be fully free, or self-governing.

This idea of independence provided the foundation for the new society that the revolutionaries of 1776 envisioned for the nation. Monarchies and aristocratic governments of the past had been able to survive and gain compliance through coercion and fear. The new world was to be different. Alluding to "all men," first of all, the revolutionaries meant that it was not simply the nobility or gentry who were worthy of independence and self-government, but *common* ordinary men as well. Although they referred narrowly only to white men,[10] the founders' belief that ordinary men were worthy of independence and self-government was itself an unprecedented idea. Elsewhere and over the ages, common men had been looked upon and treated very much like cattle. The idea of self-government based on the common man, however, raised the very real question of how such a government could survive. Tactics of control such as fear and coercion, typical of most governments throughout history, contradicted the very idea of a self-government composed of ordinary people.

To the revolutionaries of 1776, the survival of a free republican government depended upon the character of the citizenry. As Benjamin Franklin observed, "Only a virtuous people are capable of freedom."[11] Virtue, to classical republicans, meant in part the ability of an individual citizen to think and be willing to act in the public interest and for the good of the whole rather than out of private and narrow interest. Citizens could not be virtuous by definition if they either were economically dependent upon another individual, and thus subject to another's will, or were destitute, and thus necessarily self-interested. In the eyes of the revolutionaries, therefore, independence was an essential condition of virtue; a virtuous citizenry, in turn, was vital to the survival and success of self-government and a free republican society.

Because virtue and the moral integrity required for successful republican society relied upon independence, it was clear that the conditions to attain independence ought to be broadly available to citizens. The historian David Brion Davis, himself quoting from the historian Drew McCoy, described the vision held by the revolutionaries in his Massey Lectures at Harvard University in 1989: "Above all this republican America was to be characterized by an unprecedented degree of social equality, whereby even the poorest man would at least be secure, economically competent, and independent."[12]

This is not to say that the Founding Fathers believed that citizens deserved independence as an actual result or outcome; they were entitled only to the *opportunity* to attain it. The result or outcome, in terms of the requisite living standard, needed to be earned. This would depend upon the citizen's use of his own skill and effort. Given an individual's access to the necessary means to independence, a rather ordinary level of work and skill normally sufficed during the Revolutionary era to attain a frugal and yet socially acceptable living standard.[13] For competency and independence to require *exceptional* expenditures of time and levels of skill would contradict a vision asserting the worth of the ordinary man, as would demands leaving little or no time for self-development or for participation in the life of one's community or family.

The revolutionaries knew, of course, that classical history was strewn with the examples of failed republics that had succumbed to corrupt leaders and citizenries. They knew, too, that the odds they faced against success. They knew, too, that the republic they envisioned could not long endure the wretched impoverishment of the laboring masses then prevalent in England, France, and elsewhere in Europe. Such conditions were antithetical in every aspect to the development of morality and virtue; their corruptive power was dangerously corrosive to freedom. Most of the revolutionaries who had read Aristotle agreed that poverty was the great enemy of democracy. Jefferson frequently compared Europe and America, viewing with special dread the large number of European workers who had been driven on to hard labor, poverty, and ignorance, able "barely to sustain a scanty and miserable life,"[14] he said. "The want of food and clothing necessary to sustain life," Jefferson warned, "has begotten a depravity of morals, a dependence and corruption, which renders them an undesirable accession to a country whose morals are sound."[15] Franklin's tour of the British Isles in 1771, too, had shocked his sensibilities. The economic conditions of the common people there, he said, left them "miserable inhabitants," little better than "savages."[16] The comfortable independence of freeholders in America was a far preferable foundation for society, he believed, and one far less likely to become riddled with corruption in the manner of England's. "By 1775," Drew McCoy reports, "Franklin suggested that the separation of the colonies from the cancerous corruption of 'this old rotten state' had become necessary not only to preserve political liberty, but also in a much broader sense, to secure the basis for a productive and prosperous republican political economy in America."[17]

Despite the risks, there was reason for the revolutionaries to hope that America might prove an exception, at least over the foreseeable future, to the past history of republican demise from the corrosive influence of dependency and poverty. This was because the economic opportunity necessary for independence existed in abundance in America, or so many believed. John Adams in 1787 described America as a country "where the means and opportunities for luxury are so easy and so plenty."[18] Opportunity was so vast, Franklin believed, that citizens would have little reason to become jealous of immigrants.[19] Twenty years following the end of the Revolution, Jefferson wrote Madison that American workers in manufacturing "are as much at their ease, as independent and moral as our agricultural inhabitants, and they will continue to be so as long as there are vacant lands for them to resort to; because whenever it shall be attempted by the other classes to reduce them to the minimum of subsistence, they will quit their trades and go to laboring the earth."[20] It was equally reasonable for tenant farmers to hope that they would own their own land someday.[21] In his first inaugural address, Jefferson claimed that in this chosen country there was "room enough for our descendants to the thousandth and the thousandth generation."[22] Three decades later, de Tocqueville began his extraordinary book on America noting that the single most distinctive thing about the new nation was the degree to which a general equality of condition existed here.[23]

The idea of independence as understood by the revolutionaries implied not simply the limited right of equal opportunity for citizens, although surely it encompassed this right. Opportunity is equal when it is open to all citizens regardless of birth or station, when no artificial barriers to opportunity exist. Equal opportunity becomes a concern, for example, when opportunity itself is limited. If it is limited, opportunity must then go to some and not to others, based on grounds of merit, not on arbitrary considerations. However, the revolutionaries had something more in mind when they spoke of independence. It was inimical to successful republican governance for citizens to be closed out of the opportunity necessary for independence. With respect to independence, that is, opportunity needed to be plentiful, not limited. There should be enough opportunity for all, or nearly all. Absent opportunity, and the power to act on it, individuals could not be independent or truly free to attain independence. For nominal freedom, without the ability or power to use it, was not freedom at all.

The legacy of this view went back as far as John Locke. "So that liberty," Locke wrote, "is not an idea belonging to volition, or preferring; but to the person having the power of doing, or forebearing to do, according as the mind shall choose or direct. Our idea of liberty reaches as far as that power, and no farther."[24] It was in this sense that the revolutionaries believed in a rough equality of condition—that, at minimum, citizens ought to have the power to gain and maintain competency and independence. Not a guarantee of income or livelihood, but a base-line level of opportunity plentiful enough for everyone: the opportunity for a household to attain at least a comfortable subsistence if a person worked for it through means that were under the person's own control. In the view of many of the revolutionaries, the success and survival of the republic they envisioned would hang in the balance.

Barely had the Revolution commenced, though, when a bevy of new considerations began to influence American thinking about many of the practicalities of republican government.

For one, the revolutionaries' confidence that self-government could rest on the ability of independent citizens to act out of a sense of public virtue and not in the interest of narrow advancement soon came into question. George Washington, for many at the time the living embodiment of the ideal of virtue, served as a model and a powerful symbol of its possibility, but most revolutionaries fell far short of his example: "Anyone could see," the historian Charles Royster observed, "that the revolutionaries' own conduct did not conform to their image of Washington."[25] Contributions to the Revolution often hinged on self-interest; "they made considerable profit from the war when they could."[26] European subsidies and loans often were expended not on materials for war but on luxuries for private use, a goodly amount of which was purchased from Britain itself.[27] Seeking primarily their own material advancement, many men avoided service in the regular Continental army. If at all, they participated instead as privateers or briefly as substitutes in the militia because the pay and physical conditions were better.[28] In turn, the regular army was forced to rely heavily upon the lower economic strata for its recruits.[29] Revolutionary leaders thus had cause to conclude that for many in the American middle and upper strata, narrow self-interest had become the rule.[30] Washington himself grew pessimistic about the existence of a level of public virtue sufficient to provide the foundation for successful self-government.[31]

In addition, a deep economic downturn developed during the 1780s as the war was coming to a close. Unemployment and poverty worsened in the towns. Unsettling political and economic times prompted eruptions of political unrest and violence, including Shays' Rebellion in Massachusetts in 1786–87. Daniel Shays—himself a veteran and former captain in the Revolutionary army—led a successful protest to suspend judicial proceedings on hundreds of farm foreclosures in which an unruly and riotous mob surrounded the civil courts, then moved on to menace the criminal courts and federal arsenals. Shays' Rebellion became intricately interwoven into the background of what ultimately grew into the Constitutional Convention.

Finally, the republicanism of the revolutionaries had arisen largely in a precommercial agricultural economy based mostly on self-supporting or nearly self-supporting landed holdings, but this precommercial economy was on the wane. In states such as Massachusetts, a commercial market economy was already dominant in the mid-1780s, and commercial trade—and with it manufacturing and paid labor—would continue to rise.[32]

Views about republicanism and the opportunity for independence had to adapt to these profoundly changing conditions. The Revolutionary ideal of independence and virtue was reshaped, slowly, to fit the new and growing commercial economy—an economy with relatively fewer households in ownership of self-supporting property—that increasingly defined relationships among people. The reduction of ownership of self-supporting property, to the revolutionaries, meant a reduction in the independence of households; and such reduction in independence, along with the possibility of poverty, could be expected to weaken the premises upon which they believed virtuous action and a successful and safe republic relied. In the eyes of the revolutionaries, virtue involved an individual's contribution to the common good of the society by way of actions that were in the public interest. This republican idea of virtue, dominant when the colonists struggled to free themselves from England, evolved gradually "into a more modern meaning that put a premium on the productive industry of the active citizen,"[33] whether or not the citizen was a property owner and in control of the means of production. Work, production, and their commercial exchange became the way for the citizen to contribute to the welfare of the whole and thus to the public good. Also, productive work fostered a range of other virtues indispensable to the success of society and republican values, such as discipline, diligence, effort and industriousness, self-control, and responsibility.

In turn, industrious and disciplined application of one's labor, including paid work, was expected to be sufficiently well rewarded as to lead to the ability to become self-supporting and attain a decent living. According to Horace Greeley, "Every person willing to work shall assuredly have work to do, and the just reward of that work in the articles most essential to his sustenance and comfort."[34] With perseverance, mobility would also result from hard work. "Our paupers of to-day, thanks to free labor, are our yeomen and merchants of tomorrow," *The New York Times* said in 1857,[35] echoing Benjamin Franklin's claim of seventy-five years earlier that "if they are poor (in America), they first begin as Servants or Journeymen, and if they are sober, industrious, and frugal, they soon become Masters, establish themselves in Business, marry, raise families, and become respectable Citizens."[36] By diligent application of means under one's control, and particularly one's own labor, households would be able to attain a decent living and move ahead. Virtuous behavior and a dignified economic livelihood were each seen as essential to the other, and also to the common good, just as the revolutionaries had seen them at the nation's birth.

For this idea to succeed, of course, opportunity had to be plentiful and options or choice had to exist.[37] Jefferson, Adams, and Franklin presumed that the American frontier would provide inexhaustible supplies of opportunity for many decades to come, and later observers continued to find its availability to be characteristic of, and unique to, America. Still, the existence of plentiful opportunity was not simply an end in itself but a means to a more important goal: the maintenance and survival of a moral republic through the personal virtues that successful striving for economic competency and independence encouraged in the populace, and the avoidance of the indigency and economic inequality that throughout history had crippled and destroyed republics elsewhere.

In this manner, the growth of a commercial economy, through its creation of opportunity, could prove a reinforcement to republican values. Although most classical republicans were suspicious of the spread of a commercial mentality, there were some revolutionaries, such as Franklin and Adams, who saw in the commercial spirit a spur rather than a threat to virtue. Revolutionary republicans had initially assumed a strong connection between virtue and independence, but experience in the struggle against England had taught that virtue among citizens could easily succumb to self-interest. Virtue was a developed characteristic. Self-interest, on the other hand, was a force of nature. To men such as Franklin, commerce offered opportunities to bring self-interested behavior into alignment with the public good by encouraging the virtues of hard work, perseverance, and responsibility. "Is not the Hope of one day being able to purchase and enjoy Luxuries a great Spur to Labour and Industry?" Franklin asked.[38] There was little reason for citizens either to improve their skill or to increase their effort and work beyond what was necessary for a comfortable subsistence unless they could exchange the surpluses for sale on commodities enabling them to advance their material well-being.

A growing market and thriving commerce made such exchanges possible, but also required encouraging Americans to enjoy luxuries, and a standard of living, that reached beyond a comfortable subsistence. Among yeoman farmers, the lure of such luxuries could serve as an incentive to produce surpluses for sale on the market, instead of importing the luxuries from abroad, which could in turn support useful work in native manufactures for Americans in the towns.

A thriving commerce, opening up possibilities of advancement beyond independence, would reinforce the virtues of work and diligence. Expanded commercial markets, moreover, could foster greater agricultural prosperity—helping to promote peaceful political processes among farmers, a need that had become readily apparent from the turbulent and sometimes violent reaction, like Shays' Rebellion, to the growth of farm foreclosures in the countryside during the aftermath of the Revolution. A thriving commerce could operate as well to relieve the spread of unemployment in the towns that arose following the Revolution. "Most of our political evils," James Madison wrote to Jefferson in the early spring of 1787, "may be traced to our commercial ones, as most of our moral may to our political."[39] Indeed, Madison believed that the rights of property deserved utmost protection partly because they were essential to the furtherance of commerce that he considered pivotal to prosperity and the public good.[40] To survive, republican governance required not simply conditions for economic competency and independence but also a generally prospering economy that would facilitate material advancement.

James Madison is the founder most closely associated with the introduction of principles of rational self-interest into American political thinking. Virtue, to Madison, involved the willingness of an individual to respect the personal and property rights of other citizens and to act with allegiance to republican processes of government. In a republic, Madison believed, the rational self-interested citizen should always be supportive of virtuous behavior because of the personal rights that republican governance would secure for everyone—rights such as freedom of opinion, freedom of speech, and freedom from arbitrary arrest and imprisonment. These rights were of such significance, in Madison's view, that all individuals had an overriding self-interest in their protection, and thus in the preservation of republican political institutions, whether the individual owned property and was independent or not and whether the individual was economically prosperous or not.

Whatever the merits of its logic, however, Madison also recognized that this theory of self-interested virtue had a number of serious weaknesses. For one, it depended upon the institutions operating in such manner as actually to secure the rights of all in an impartial and effective way. Questions about the validity of this assumption were raised in Madison's mind before the new Constitution had reached its fourth birthday. In 1791 the federal government created a national bank that operated, in Madison's view, in a high-handed and wholly partial fashion on behalf of moneyed interests and wealthy speculators. In many cases, the very members of government became the benefactors. Madison believed that such decisions, and the process that led to them, were detrimental to the interests of the populace as a whole and the poor in particular. If Madison understood that self-interest could at times be aligned with the welfare of republican institutions, he also recognized that the actual takeover of these institutions by partial interests would undermine the institutions and the Republic. The development of a system of checks and balances, along with other devices, in the attempt to prevent partial interests from gaining dominance had preoccupied him for this very reason.

There was also a second, equally fundamental problem with the proposition that self-interest could serve to sustain republican institutions, and Madison well recognized and understood it, too. Despite his conviction that fair and effective protection of the personal rights of all gave even the propertyless and poor a self-interested stake in the maintenance of republican institutions, he recognized that human emotion might make it appear otherwise, especially concerning matters of economic status and well-being. Without the economic competency and independence of the largest possible proportion of the population, he believed, a republic would become vulnerable. The economically competent and independent, having at stake not only personal but also property rights and a minimally decent standard of living, had more reason than the poor to preserve a republic. Madison wrote: "The best distribution (of occupations) is that which would most favor health, virtue, intelligence and competency in the greatest number of citizens," and he went on to say: "It is needless to add to these objects, liberty and safety. The first is presupposed by them. The last must result from them."[41] Similarly, he observed, "The class of citizens who provide at once their own food and their own raiment, may be viewed as the most truly independent and happy. They are more: they are the best basis of public liberty, and the strongest bulwark of public safety. It follows, that the greater the proportion of this class to the whole society, the more free . . . and the more happy must be the society itself."[42] Nothing was more clear to Madison than that the rights of property and the safety and stability of society would become increasingly vulnerable to the degree that the populace was incapable of independence. As he had written in his historic *Federalist* No. 10, "The most common and durable source of factions has been the various and unequal distribution of property."[43] If a great inequality of property existed and was allowed to persist, Madison knew that the blessings of personal liberty would come to seem dubious. No republican arrangements could be devised, he believed, that could long withstand the spread of feelings of indigence. The opportunity to attain economic independence was essential. By the early 1790s, concerned that the deep antagonisms dividing the wealthy and the poor could ultimately become disruptive and destabilizing, Madison advised that the laws of the government be used to "reduce extreme wealth towards a state of mediocrity, and raise extreme indigence toward a state of comfort."[44]

Madison understood that even if poverty did not involve any loss of personal rights, the powerful psychological effects growing out of the inability to rise above feelings of indigency, in the absence of sufficient opportunities to move ahead, could not be ignored. Ultimately, they would spawn unrest and violence among segments of the poor—as they had prior to the Constitutional Convention—that would create social instability and threaten the personal and property rights of others. Further growth in the numbers of poor in the populace would worsen the situation still more; in larger numbers, the poor might be able to gain control and use the power of government itself to attack and abrogate the rights of property. Only two courses of action could redress these eventualities. One was through the use of physical armed coercion—sheer force—against the poor. This would entail costly expenditures; but even more, the use and spread of such force would impinge upon the very liberties that republicanism was intended to protect. The alternative, which Madison urged, was to create a government that had effective power, first, to promote the creation of opportunity for all and, second, to moderate economic inequality at the extremes. Without these policies, Madison believed, a republican society was doomed either to civil unrest and instability or, in reaction, to the anathema of the widespread use of physical force.

A popular libertarian view of the founders' attitudes about government claims that men such as Jefferson and Madison believed that government's proper role was strictly a negative one, confined to the protection of personal and property rights, and that economic and social engineering went beyond the proper bounds of government. Nothing could be further from the truth. The Revolutionary leaders and framers of the Constitution believed that the maintenance of republican liberty and safety required certain economic and social conditions that the government should properly try to foster. To create the economic foundation they considered necessary for a secure republic, they did not shy away from urging an active government—a government active not simply in protecting the rights of persons and property but also in promoting economic opportunity and reducing disadvantage within the citizenry. Madison, as we have seen, believed it was appropriate for government to enact laws that would raise the indigent toward a state of comfort and reduce excesses of wealth. Jefferson, too, in his notes on the Constitution of Virginia, called upon government to use its power over public lands to grant fifty acres of land to any household that had no property, an amount of acreage that would easily assure a comfortable subsistence given an ordinary input of work and skill.[45] He elaborated in a letter to Madison in 1785:

Whenever there is in any country, uncultivated lands and unemployed poor, it is clear that the laws of property have been so far extended as to violate a natural right. The earth is given as a common stock for man to labour and live on. If, for encouragement of industry we allow it to be appropriated, we must take care that other employment be furnished to those excluded from the appropriation. If we do not the fundamental right to labour the earth returns to the unemployed.[46]

It was common among the founders to believe that government ought to devise laws, respectful of the rights of property, that would encourage the division of land into small quantities so as to enable the broad citizenry to become owners of property.[47] To the revolutionaries, whose fervent desire it was to instill and reinforce republican virtues, competency and independence "were the necessary antidote to corruption."[48]

Most preferred that the government shy away from granting income to individuals directly, but wanted government to help expand and enlarge opportunity generally so that it would be available and accessible to citizens acting on their own initiative. The possibility of establishing a strong, active government necessary to expand opportunity loomed large in the drive to amend the Articles of Confederation and in the ultimate outcome of the Constitutional Convention. It seemed to many that securing control from native peoples and Europeans of the immense tracts of fertile land stretching to the banks of the Mississippi and to the West beyond—and, moreover, opening European trade markets to surpluses fashioned from the land by industrious American farmers—could expand prosperity indefinitely. Both would benefit substantially from a stronger and more active central government. Only a powerful central government could successfully face down Spanish and French negotiators for control of the Mississippi River, essential to American settlement of the West. Only a strong central government could wrest control of the land beyond the Mississippi from the French (soon achieved, somewhat by surprise, through the Louisiana Purchase). Moreover, only an active central government could support the construction and defense of roads and other improvements needed to ensure the free and unfettered trade of goods from the western lands into the American states so as to generate commerce and tie the frontier economically to the nation. Finally, only the power of a determined central government, able with authority to deny European access to American markets, had any chance of opening European markets to the purchase of American farm surpluses. These reasons as much as any others, all tied firmly to the goals of economic independence and advancement for Americans, paved the way for the nation to move from the confederal government to the strengthened and more assertive central government that the Constitutional Convention created and the thirteen American states adopted from 1787 to 1789.

At the core of republican ideas during the Revolution and the writing of the Constitution lay a conception of the material foundations needed to instill and preserve republican virtues. Both Jeffersonian and Madisonian republicans believed that the survival of a stable republic and the inculcation of its moral values hinged upon the existence of economic conditions making enough opportunity available to citizens to enable them to attain a living of at least minimal comfort through means under their own control, lifting them above both indigence and dependency upon others. Madisonian republicans went even further, believing that prosperous commercial conditions were also essential in order to give already independent citizens the incentive and ability to advance their economic well-being by intensifying their practice of the virtues associated with work, thus reinforcing a republican morality still more.

To the founders, the provision of opportunity for independence and advancement was a first principle upon which the maintenance of other fundamental political values rested. It was essential to the building of a nation of virtuous people who could simultaneously be free, secure, and able to enjoy a basic equality of respect and feeling of inclusion. Were they to assess the state of the nation today, very likely nothing would weigh more heavily in their judgment than the extent to which what we today call the American Dream survives. They would ask how well the nation measures up to the precept that the opportunity to attain economic independence and advancement be available to all citizens. In their eyes, the answer would reveal much about the moral strength, health, and stability of the country to which they gave birth. To them, the answer would measure the essence of what philosopher Michael Sandel calls "the political economy of citizenship."[49] The answer, James Madison said, would tell them no less than how happy a society the nation they invented had become.

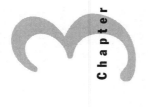

Chapter 3

IS THERE ANOTHER BOTTOM LINE?

In formulating their ideas for the new nation, the founders undeniably showed uncommon wisdom and insight. Changes of enormous magnitude have taken place over the past two centuries, however. These changes raise powerful questions as to the weight we ought to give today to the founders' beliefs. Apart from the founders' insistent warnings about the effects of constricted opportunity on the health and continued success of a republic, certain fundamental moral principles lay behind the importance they attached to the idea of independence. Do these principles, proclaimed by Thomas Jefferson two centuries ago, still hold? How much should they continue to influence us today, particularly when set alongside other compelling moral ideals that may be more in keeping with the requirements of contemporary society?

The founders' beliefs about independence developed in the context of a precommercial economy where independence significantly overlapped with self-sufficiency; where much of what a typical household produced was for itself. With the subsequent growth and eventual dominance of the market economy, what workers produced needed to find a buyer. Production was increasingly for someone else rather than for oneself. With this transformation, issues of reciprocity and desert—whether each party to a transaction is getting a fair and equivalent return—entered squarely into the picture.

The idea that a person ought to receive in reasonable proportion to what he or she gives or contributes is a compelling moral framework that has had powerful influence both throughout history and across numerous cultures.[1] Many Americans today believe that the outcomes of the commercial free market reflect the worth of individuals' contributions, as manifested in popular expressions like "You get what you earn" and "You get what you pay for." It may seem to follow, then, that a person's ability to attain competency and independence ought to rest on the person's ability to make an appropriate contribution through the private market. But to what degree should we allow the marketplace to rule on matters having to do with competency and independence? If they conflict, should the market's distribution of returns prevail, or should the conditions necessary for competency and independence be given priority? To what degree should the nation rely upon the outcomes of the free market?

One weakness of the market as a mechanism of fair exchange is that the market takes the existing possessions of individuals as a given. At any particular point in time, what an individual is able to purchase and receive from the market is, of course, a function of the individual's income and wealth. As a consequence, the ability of the free market to reflect exchanges that are fair depends upon whether each person's income, or buying power, itself has been fairly gained—that is, whether the present distribution of income is right and just. This is necessarily questionable not merely in light of the illegitimate appropriations of property and labor that have occurred historically[2] but based on similar considerations in the present day.[3]

As a result, it is very difficult to justify the current income distribution on the ground that it has been fairly gained. The philosopher Brian Barry observes:[4]

The glaring limitation of justice as reciprocity is that it can say nothing about the initial control over natural resources. Once ownership rights are assigned, justice as reciprocity can tell us about fair trading. But it is silent on the crucial first stage. Theorists who wish to place fair exchange at the center of their conceptions of justice, from John Locke to James Buchanan and Robert Nozick, have always recognized that some other kind of theory has to be brought in to get things started or that one must simply be agnostic about the initial distribution of resources.

Once things get started, however, many people believe that the free market addresses the issue of fair exchange about as well as it is possible to do. A market is free when individuals voluntarily opt to trade goods and services. Individuals freely decide what is of value to them and of how much value. If they elect to trade goods and services, they decide to do so because they value what they get more than what they give. Unless one side has been deceived about the trade by the other, each side to the voluntary trade should end up better off than it was before. How much an individual receives from others in a free market should be a function of how much that individual has added or contributed to the welfare of others, as determined by how much others are willing to give the individual in return. In theory, free market outcomes will reward in accordance with the marginal contribution (called the marginal product) that each worker makes.

Yet few seriously contend that the market rewards marginal productivity perfectly. The most that can be said, according to economists such as Milton Friedman, is that the market *tends* toward such outcomes; other economists, such as Friedrich Hayek, claim that not even this tendency necessarily exists.[5] Much production within a company is a highly collaborative process involving dozens and even thousands of people. How does the Ford Motor Company, internally, determine the marginal contribution made to its product and sales by a computer programmer as opposed to a design analyst, or by these personnel as opposed to a vice president in charge of marketing? Exactly the same work in different companies may be rewarded with significantly different wages by those companies.[6] The return to one employee within a firm will depend upon the quality of the work done by other employees, including the quality of the job done by management. When Toyota and Honda moved production facilities into the United States, their experiences led many to conclude that the problem with the American automobile industry was not so much that its workers had become unproductive as that the views of management and the techniques it used were outdated.[7] Speaking about American industry generally, W. Edwards Demning, the highly acclaimed consultant to many Japanese firms, observed: "Loss of market, and resulting unemployment, are not foreordained. They are not inevitable. They are man-made. The basic cause of sickness in American industry and resulting unemployment is failure of top management to manage. . . . The problem is where to find good management. It would be a mistake to export American management to a friendly country.

Poor management may be part of the answer to the following conundrum: Why, notwithstanding a 34 percent rise in the productivity of manufacturing workers during the 1980s and their superior absolute level of productivity as compared to that of the workers of any other nation, did the real wages of manufacturing workers in this country fail on average to rise at all over those ten years? Throughout the period, American manufacturing workers were paid considerably less than their equivalents in most of the other industrialized countries. As economist Richard Freeman of Harvard pointed out, "Given comparable levels of productivity, American workers are a low-wage bargain in the developed world."[10] With workers absolutely superior in productivity and paid less relative to productivity than in other nations like Germany or France, one might surmise that the real profits of our manufacturing companies would have been pretty good. But they weren't. Instead, the profits of manufacturing firms turned southward over the decade.[11]

Many glaring individual discrepancies in earnings are hard to justify according to any commonsense definition of payment for contribution and value—beyond the tautological one that individual reward was "determined by the market." Scores of major league ballplayers and movie and other media stars make in the millions of dollars a year; according to *Forbes* magazine, at least forty entertainers earned more than $20 million annually in 1993–94. Of these, the least-paid, Roseanne, earned $23 million[12]—more than the entire physics faculties at MIT and Harvard combined.[13] At the other end of the scale, American garment workers, who are among the most productive in the world (nearly twice as productive as workers in places like Bangladesh), take fourteen minutes on average to manufacture a shirt. Their wages amount to about $1.76 per shirt.[14] At that rate, it would require the manufacture of more than 13 million shirts, taking more than 1,690 productive workers a year to produce, to reach an output having a market value in labor equal to the value the market places on Roseanne's work alone.

Some speculate that lofty earnings are required in order to give incentive to people to go into highly remunerative occupations. If so, a similar argument could be made about low-paid occupations: perhaps some workers don't enter them, and instead remain unemployed, or are employed intermittently, or turn to illicit activities, because the economic incentives attached to the jobs are so low that they don't support a minimally respectable living. If higher pay motivates economic behavior, the same presumably applies to low-paid jobs. Yet the truth of even this reasonable proposition has its limits. The entertainment and sports worlds never were wanting for aspirants even in the days when they paid next to nothing, and many positions of great responsibility today don't require stratospheric salaries to attract the interest and commitment of enormously capable personnel. While the market may bid up the salaries of corporate CEOs as well as of some physicians, lawyers, brokers, and accountants into the millions of dollars, private foundations, charities, and the judiciary, not to mention Congress and the administration, find similarly skilled and talented people for a fraction of the price.

Considerations such as these raise questions about what we really mean when we use terms such as "worth," "contribution," and "value" in talking about how the free market's distribution of income conforms with desert and reciprocity. According to the notion of desert, an exchange between people means that a person has done something of equivalent worth or value for another. But when we say "worth" or "value" in the context of a market, what do we mean? In the context of the market and its morality, it is perfectly acceptable to seek to get something not for what you think it is worth, but for the very least you can get it. You probably won't pay more than you consider it's worth, of course; however, if you can, you might pay less—even a lot less—than you think it's worth. The market, then, is not talking about worth in any absolute sense tied to difficulty of work, hours of labor, or even more intangible notions of the value either the seller or buyer might see in something. Rather, the worth of something in the market—its price—is a mechanistic notion, merely the intersection of supply and demand.

I know a rancher in Arizona. He owns a guest ranch, a peaceful place built on a stretch of flat land along a lazy creek sheltered by tall cottonwood trees and bordered on either side by the walls of a steep canyon. I was talking to him one early fall day as we were walking along a bank of boulders that lined the creek like a high beach—not natural, but put in place by a laborer the ranch had hired. José Baraza was his name. He took massive rocks that had populated the creek bed and placed them in wide, deep piles for more than five hundred feet all along each side of the meandering bank, preventing both soil erosion and the flooding that had regularly gutted the small cabins, making the ranch worthless for paying guests. The work took José the best part of a year, but by now the bank of boulders had held up perfectly for eight years and made possible the transformation of a cattle ranch that barely produced a living into a commercially successful guest ranch. What was José paid for his contribution? The going rate for a day laborer was near minimum wage. At that rate, José received (in 1995 dollars) somewhere around $8,500 for ten months' work plus Social Security tax. What was the value of his work? Had my friend had to pay three or four times as much at the time, I imagine he would have done so without a blink of an eye. But there were plenty of laborers looking for such work. Supply and demand, not the true value of the labor in the eyes of the recipient, determined the pay José Baraza received.

The same is true for the idea of earning—it, too, gains a different meaning in the language of the market than common parlance gives to it. We often hear it said, "I *earned* that money, so I have a right to it." The idea of earning here does not mean simply that I got what the market will bear (the intersection of supply and demand). The idea of earning, in common parlance, has something to do with the degree of effort that was expended and with the difficulty of that effort.

In the language of the market, the notion of earning easily becomes transformed (and cheapened) if, even though this goes unstated, it really comes to mean that the extent and difficulty of one's efforts are validly measured by whatever pay the market will bear. Consider the example of Ollie North. There are many marines who have made little money but have performed with as much courage, valor, and patriotism as he, and paid at least as great a price. When the Iran-Contra scandal came to public knowledge in the late 1980s, North's fame spread and he became widely sought as a speaker. He reportedly made as much as $25,000 per speech. North says he sees nothing wrong with this: "I earned it," he says. "Every one of those speeches was a night away from home."[15] Even here North is acknowledging, implicitly, that the concept of earning requires a justification having something to do with the effort or sacrifices required.

A civilian counterexample to Ollie North is thirty-three-year-old Willie Kimble, who receives about $7 an hour, or around $14,000 for a year's full-time work at forty hours a week. As reported by journalist Tony Horwitz, Willie hitches incoming birds to shackles at a poultry plant in Mississippi. During eight hours' work, he'll hitch twelve thousand birds at a rate of nearly one bird every two seconds, minute after minute, hour after hour. The job takes great strength and endurance. It is not simply because of the unrelenting fast pace of the job. It is also that the live birds struggle hard, they peck, scratch, and defecate. Kimble's arms are cut and bruised all over, his hands solidly calloused. This job exposes him to a rate of injury and illness of twenty-three per hundred workers a year—about double the rate for hazardous jobs like coal mining. "It's tough work and will make you sore as hell," says Jerry Duty, a chicken-processing plant manager. Willie says he keeps the job because the wages are better than at other jobs either in the plant or elsewhere in the area.[16]

What does the idea of "earning" the wage you receive mean? North was using the language of the market when he spoke. He was saying, at bottom, that "the market paid me $25,000, so I earned it." Ask Willie Kimble and he'll tell you that anyone who says he earned $25,000 for preparing and delivering one speech and spending one night on the road away from home doesn't know the real meaning of the word "earning," certainly not as experienced in the world of low-wage families. José Baraza will tell you the same. So will fast food workers. When working full-time, they may be on their feet without rest four to six hours at a stretch; the work is generally at a very rapid pace (a pace over which they exercise little control); they operate under the constant pressure of careful monitoring for precise accuracy; and they are held strictly accountable for errors. At the end of a long day they are left aching.[17] Contrary to the conventional image of the job, it is tough, physically exhausting work if done full-time. And the pay is generally near minimum wage, less than $11,000 for year-round employment. No accounting of the concept of earning that puts a value on effort or even the difficulty of the conditions under which the work is carried out can explain how people such as Willie Kimble, José Baraza, fast food workers, and millions of others like them receive for a whole year's labor less than half of the pay others receive in a single *day*.

No argument has been offered to refute the common meanings of words like "contribution," "worth," and "earn" or to show that the common meanings of these words are somehow misdirected. Nor has the principle of supply and demand been shown to provide a philosophically superior meaning. There is no reason to accept supply and demand as a conclusive measure of either the value of people's contributions to others or of the degree of effort they have expended.

Let us presume, however, that the market did result in a reasonable level of return that was commensurate with commonly held definitions of terms such as "contribution," "worth," and "earn." Even then, there are crucial values to which the society is and ought to be deeply committed that would not be taken into account, such as the fundamental moral equality of persons.

Americans rightly reject the idea that only those who make a contribution—and only to the degree they do (or are likely to) contribute—deserve any return. This suggests that the millions of people who contribute very little or nothing as the market defines it—the mentally handicapped, the severely disabled, and the ill, for examples—are useless, expendable. Such people are considered deserving of assistance from the society precisely because we value the notion that they are morally equal, and therefore worthy of a respectful level of acceptance, support, and inclusion without their making a fully commensurate contribution. [18]

These are all examples of people whose condition falls outside of their own personal control. What then of individuals who are unable to make a contribution because they have no opportunity to do so due to factors beyond their control? Don't they logically deserve a response from society granting them similar acceptance and inclusion? The principle of equal moral worth involves valuing the fundamental interests of each human being as a moral agent and ensuring that the meeting of these fundamental interests, wherever possible, remains within the individual's capacity to control. Among the interests fundamental to individuals is inclusion and acceptance within one's society.[19] Within the value scheme that regards each individual as morally equal, ensuring the availability of opportunity to attain a respectful level of acceptance and inclusion in the society must be given precedence over considerations associated solely with the capacity to contribute.[20]

By no means is this to say that society has an obligation to offer handouts to able-bodied people who will not work. Society does have an obligation, however, to ensure that *opportunity* is available in sufficient supply to able-bodied people who are willing to work so that they can provide a minimally dignified living or better for themselves, certainly in a society where attaining such a living serves as a measure of basic respect and inclusion. Society also has an obligation to assist the unemployed who are willing to work over a reasonable transitional period to enable them to prepare for or locate jobs. If sufficient opportunity to earn a decent living truly is available,[21] private organizations may still wish to assist able individuals who will not work, but society as a collectivity has no obligation to do so.[22]

In addition to the proposition of equal moral worth, other values of considerable importance to Americans have little or no place within a society based on the idea of mere desert. Among them is the high priority Americans attach to good character, and particularly to the work ethic. The columnist Robert J. Samuelson reminds us that "the American ethic has always held that individual effort [is] valued and rewarded."[23] Suppose the low wages received by José Baraza and Willie Kimble and the many others like them did in fact reflect the precise worth of what they contributed. This fails to take into account the fact that they are hard, steady, and persevering workers, highly virtuous people in terms that society greatly reveres. It is one thing to say that the society should reward those individuals who make substantial contributions far more handsomely than it rewards others who may work as hard but make a lesser contribution. It is quite another thing for the same society to say that it is willing to leave genuinely hardworking and persevering people unable to attain a minimally respectable living, enough of a living even to put a frugal person within the margins of the mainstream. A society cannot do this without sending the message that hard work and perseverance are little valued in themselves, that traits Americans have considered fundamental virtues actually may yield very little.

Some kinds of work—work as a day laborer, a poultry processor, a fast-food server, a bottling plant worker, and the like—are held in low regard even though they require the ability to do demanding physical work or to perform accurately in routinized, fast-paced jobs for long hours, day after day with no end in sight. Like the aristocrats our forebears rebelled against in 1776, large numbers of Americans have come to see many kinds of work as beneath them, as undeserving of decent pay. Such views only amplify the unintended message that hard work and effort are not important qualities in themselves.

And then there are the numerous highly valued human activities that the market hardly recognizes at all. No one would deny that good parenting makes a substantial contribution to the health and welfare of society, yet it receives little from society in return except public education and a very modest tax break. Instead, the economic mechanisms of reward may actually leave good parents who work year-round full-time in productive jobs with too little to afford a minimally respectable standard of living.

The market at best only *tends* to reward the level of an individual's contribution, and then only with respect to those activities incorporated within the market. In fact, many workers are not receiving wages fully commensurate with their contribution. Some are receiving more than they contributed, others less, at times quite a bit less. On these grounds alone, market outcomes should not be taken and legitimized as conclusive, as a final arbiter. Moreover, to take the level of contribution as the sole value or objective itself conflicts with the idea that human beings are morally equal and neglects the importance of work, effort, self-discipline, and perseverance as virtues separate and apart from the exact worth they contribute. To the founders of the nation, these values—the moral equality of individuals and the virtues of work, effort, self-discipline, and perseverance—were vital.[24]

We often hear it said, in defense of the morality of market arrangements, that low-wage workers and the poor do not have to stay that way: they remain free to choose otherwise and to earn a decent living and work their way up by training themselves for and finding better jobs. They can determine their own fate.

This *is* a powerful argument, but only if it is true.[25] If people don't have access to the resources for training or if, even when they are trained, the opportunities are not there for a large number of them to make a decent living and move ahead, then the claim that their fate is self-imposed loses its force. As John Locke observed, to be free to undertake an action but to lack the power or the ability to do so is a contradiction in terms and a violation of the meaning of liberty.[26] One cannot be held accountable for that which is outside one's control, James Madison reminded us.[27] This is one reason why the idea that enough opportunity exist for all is itself a moral bottom line and why it has been a driving force and achieved such resonance in American thinking ever since Jefferson's ringing proposition ushered in the revolution and the birth of our nation.[28]

POSTSCRIPT

The idea that the opportunity to attain a respectful level of acceptance and inclusion in the society should be available to all follows from the precept that regards each individual as morally equal. In addition, this same conclusion might follow were individuals in no way interested in the moral equality of others but merely concerned with their own self-interest, assuming they did not know what status they themselves were likely to attain in society. That is, a case can be made that rational self-interested persons ignorant of their own capabilities and future potential would agree to enter social arrangements, or a social compact, only if it protected the right to the opportunity to attain a minimally acceptable living according to the standards of basic decency and respect in the society. Consider the problem in today's terms.

Suppose that being poor, despite trying, meant a high probability of living in neighborhoods that were dilapidated and violent, leading an average person to think: "I wouldn't be caught *dead* in that neighborhood." Suppose that being poor, despite trying, was likely to affect the normal mental development of one's children, since many poor children receive inferior nutrition, poor health care, and inadequate schooling, and was likely to lead to their premature death as adults. Suppose that being poor, despite trying, disposed one ultimately to see one's own self as inferior or of little value in a society forever telling its citizens that the opportunity to attain an adequate living exists for all. The word "poor" itself, as in "poor performance" or "poor result," carries the clear connotation of *failure*. Given such social constructions and the presumed opportunity to succeed, remaining poor over a sustained period of time is apt to become viewed by oneself and the larger society as the result of a profound personal defect. Suppose that being poor, despite trying, was likely to inhibit one's ability to become involved in community affairs and the processes of government that make the rules regulating one's own behavior (low self-esteem, strain and worry, and the lack of material possessions such as a telephone all tend to restrict such involvement). Suppose that being poor, despite trying, meant being subject to a system of law enforcement in which convictions for some offenses were based as much or more on income level than on the actual evidence.

Contemplating all these possible (and real) indecencies, self-interested citizens surely would be considered rational were they to want protection from them. Suppose that only a small minority of the populace were likely to become poor. The cost of ensuring sufficient opportunity to enable a small minority of the populace to raise themselves through work out of poverty and up to a level of minimal comfort would be trivial if spread among the remainder of the public. To the extent that a greater number were likely to become poor, on the other hand, the risk of experiencing poverty and the indignities associated with it would increase (becoming increasingly unacceptable to the average person). In either case, rational individuals with no knowledge of their own ultimate status or future potential would call for policies to ensure the existence, at the very least, of the opportunity to rise out of poverty.[29] The idea that opportunity should be available for all to attain decent livelihoods resonates deeply and virtually universally among Americans. That this is so may not be solely because of the idea's tie to the belief in the equal moral worth of individuals but also because of the implicit understanding that any self-interested individual would be considered rational were he or she to want such opportunity to exist.

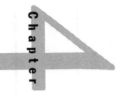

FINDING OUT ABOUT
ECONOMIC OPPORTUNITY,

The federal government has steadfastly avoided compiling any sort of reliable information about the job opportunities and pay levels available to Americans who are looking for employment or seeking better work, despite the many calls from scholars, analysts, and numerous interest groups for it to do so.[1] So has virtually every state government. The founders' convictions about the vital importance of opportunity for citizens to attain competency and independence to the health and success of a free and moral society could hardly be given less deference, as is also true of the principle of equal moral worth proclaimed by Jefferson at the nation's founding and by Lincoln at its rebirth eight decades later. Lacking direct measures, assertions about *whether or not enough opportunity for Americans actually exists* must rely largely upon indirect or anecdotal evidence, ideological belief, or a combination of the two. The same holds true for national and state employment policies, including all job-training and workfare programs. Surprising as it is, all such policies are based not upon sound evidence but rather upon what are at base presumptions about the availability of jobs, the status of those jobs (full-time or part-time, full-year or part-year), the kinds of skills those jobs require, and the amount of pay and benefits they offer. Neither the American federal and state governments nor the public at large has assembled any systematic information about the opportunities that are available and able to provide economic independence and advancement, whether nationally or on a local basis.

The nation has satisfied itself instead with a proxy measure, called the unemployment rate. Announced the first Friday of each month, often with considerable publicity, the rate of unemployment measures how many workers in the labor force have no job yet are looking for employment. At first glance, the rate of unemployment might appear to be an excellent yardstick of the level of economic opportunity available to workers. In America, having a job has historically been viewed as the equivalent or near equivalent of being self-supporting. Consequently, if nearly all workers are employed in jobs, and the rate of unemployment is low, it would seem to follow that few workers will be unable to find opportunity at least sufficient to take care of themselves. The opposite conclusion would follow if the rate of unemployment was high.

Lurking beneath the surface, however, are numerous shortcomings in the rate of unemployment as a method to measure the availability of economic opportunity. For one, the measure considers any person to be a member of the labor force and unemployed if the individual has no work but says that he or she has recently looked for a job. Yet some job seekers may be serious about looking for a job,[2] others may not be. Jobs could be readily available, as many observers contend is the case, while the unemployed remain out of work because they are extremely particular about the jobs they will accept. Some of these "job seekers" perhaps may not really want to work at all, or they may be unwilling to take entry-level jobs and make the effort necessary to work their way up. To the degree that job seekers find only a narrow range of jobs acceptable, the rate of unemployment will be inflated. To complicate matters further, some workers counted as unemployed are simply between jobs and have already secured other jobs, which they will soon take up. Their numbers, too, can inflate the unemployment rate, suggesting a lower level of opportunity than actually exists.

Yet the opposite could just as easily hold true. The government-measured rate of unemployment considers a person to be employed if he or she is working only a handful of hours a week for pay. Workers who occupy part-time jobs, working perhaps ten or twenty or thirty hours a week, are counted as employed even if they are trying to locate full-time jobs but have been unable to find them. Anywhere from 4.2 million to more than 6 million workers fell into this category yearly between 1990 and 1995—fully two-thirds the number of the measured unemployed—but all these workers were counted as employed. The rate of unemployment doesn't consider, either, the adequacy of the level of pay or benefits of the jobs that the employed—even the full-time employed—do hold. For example, the measure makes no distinction between a head of household who is paid $5.50 an hour for full-time work and a supplemental earner of a household earning that same wage or a worker earning, say, $25 or $50 an hour. Unemployment measures whether individuals have jobs or not, and nothing else.

Surely the nation's founders, with their great concern about idleness and inoccupation, would have given some attention to the unemployment rate as the government today defines and measures it. But they cared about far more than this as well, believing that competency and independence were necessary. The unit of analysis for competency and independence must be the whole household (whether the household be a family unit composed of more than one person or a unit composed of just a single individual); the unemployment rate, by contrast, takes only the individual into account. Likewise, the unemployment rate makes no reference to the level of an individual's (or household's) standard of living; any job, regardless of hours and wage level or fringe benefits, is sufficient to record a worker as employed, even if the worker lives in poverty. Yet independence assumes competency, and competency calls for individual households to be able to secure a minimally dignified level of living; to be able to attain all the necessaries of life, managing frugally, at a level considered minimally respectable within common social norms.[3]

The idea of independence also raises issues about the level of control a household has over the resources required to provide its sustenance in a commercial context, namely its own labor. Meaningful control over the use of one's own labor requires the availability of a true choice of employments[4] able to generate remuneration providing a minimally dignified living or better. Also, one's labor must be able to earn the basic living through a reasonable expenditure of effort, leaving some time for other spheres of life.[5] The unemployment rate makes no attempt to measure any of these considerations, considerations that, incidentally, comprise the minimum that independence and competency require. To Jefferson and others, independence also meant control over the work itself (possibly they would accept worker participation or codetermination in today's terminology); respectable work—that is, work that the individual and others considered respectable, which farming was; and work that required use of one's intelligence.[6]

How, then, can we find out whether enough opportunity is available in this nation enabling American families to gain and maintain independence? First, since competency and independence require the ability to achieve a minimally dignified living, or comfortable subsistence, we must be able to judge what today constitutes that level of living, what I will call the lowest and most frugal level of a mainstream standard of living:[7] a level of living able to provide all of the necessaries of life, as defined by the culture, at the lowest realistic cost and in a minimally decent manner.

Items considered necessary and minimally decent or respectable in the culture are not always essential to sheer physical survival, of course. According to Adam Smith, necessities are "not only the commodities which are indispensably necessary for the support of life, but whatever the custom of the country renders it indecent for creditable people, even of the lowest order, to be without."[8] Linen shirts and leather shoes were examples he offered for his day. A person today surely could survive in a small shack with outdoor plumbing, without electricity or hot water, and having dirt floors with no bed or any furniture, but to live this way would be considered less than creditable unless it were by choice, and perhaps not even then. It is norms of culture and not the requirements of physical survival that make such conveniences as hot running water and indoor plumbing, electricity, and furniture seem to be basic necessities of everyday living. In the minds of most Americans, the same applies to refrigerators and telephones.[9]

No universal consensus exists as to each and every particular of what does and does not constitute a necessity,[10] or at what specific level each particular ought to be attained to qualify as minimally respectable. Yet public opinion polls taken over a period of more than forty years can give us a sense of people's perceptions of the overall level of income needed to attain the minimum prevailing standard of living as they see it defined and experience it themselves within the society. Recently, representative samples of Americans have been asked by the Roper organization: "How much income per year would you say you and your family need (1) just to get by? (2) in order to live in reasonable comfort? and (3) to fulfill all your dreams?" Prior to 1988, Gallup asked representative samples of Americans: "What is the smallest amount of money a family of four needs each week to get along in this community?"[11]

In the early 1950s the smallest amount of money the public believed to be necessary was an income nearly the same as the one then arrived at by the federal government's measure of the poverty line.[12] Yet very quickly the responses of Americans to the Gallup survey questions began to rise sharply above the dollar level that became the federal government's poverty-line income. By 1970, two decades later, the poverty line amounted to an income that barely reached 60 percent of what the public considered the smallest amount needed to get along (see Table 1). Something had gone awry either in the public's responses or the government's measure of the poverty line. The responses of the public were keyed, of course, to the smallest income it took to live in the style common to that day. At the outset, in the early 1950s, fully two fifths of American households had no automobile, about a third did not have a private telephone or a television, and the homes of about a third of all Americans were dilapidated or were without running water or a private toilet and bath.[13] Only a small minority of families enjoyed such basics as a mixer or had a hot-water heater in their home. As items such as these became more customary and indeed nearly universal, the answers of the public took their cost into account, but the federal poverty line remained frozen in consumption patterns of the mid-1950s. Modified only for inflation, adjustments to the poverty line took into account changes in the price of what was considered essential in 1955,[14] but not changes in living standards occurring thereafter. The same is still true today; while the answers of the public to the Gallup and Roper questions refer to the amount of money the public perceives it takes to reach a contemporary minimum standard of living, the federal poverty line is forever arbitrarily moored to 1955. Since nothing recommends the 1955 living standard as a model or ideal for any other period, one wonders whether the federal poverty line is measuring anything very much at all any longer.

Table 1.

THE RELATION BETWEEN THE FEDERAL POVERTY LINE AND
PUBLIC OPINION ABOUT THE SMALLEST AMOUNT OF MONEY IT TAKES
A FAMILY OF FOUR TO GET ALONG OVER A YEAR (IN DOLLARS)

	Federal Poverty Line Income	Income Required According to the Public[†]	Poverty Line as a Percentage of Required Income
1950*	2,460	2,500	98.4
1960	3,022	4,238	71.3
1970	3,968	6,552	60.6
1980	8,414	13,000	64.7
1990	13,359	22,400	59.6

*The poverty line is projected back to 1950 by the Consumer Price Index.
[†]Calculated from the results of Gallup and Roper public opinion polls (see *The Public Perspective*, November/December 1994, p. 98; and *Gallup Report*, May 1986, p. 3).

In 1994 the American public responded to the Roper poll that it took a family of four about $25,000 just to get by; the federal poverty line for a family of four for that year stood at about $15,000. Suppose that in 1994 a household of two adults and two children had just enough money to feed itself on what the United States Department of Agriculture considered the smallest amount necessary to obtain a minimally healthy diet—about $88 per week; suppose the family found and rented a two-bedroom apartment meeting the government's definition of a low-cost rental unit, paying a rent of no more than $380 a month for an apartment for the four of them and no more than $130 a month on all utilities, including telephone; suppose the family owned a single intermediate-size vehicle[15] over a period of ten years and 100,000 miles, paying the average cost of about $3,700 a year to operate the vehicle, maintain it in reliable running order, insure it, and pay the cost of depreciation, and also incurred $400 in public transportation costs for a second worker; suppose the family spent $2,000 a year, including insurance premiums and co-payments, on all medical, pharmaceutical, and dental bills for the four members of the household; and suppose it kept expenditures on all clothing for two working adults and two growing children to no more than $1,000 for the year. Of course, in addition, the family would have to purchase a variety of personal items (from toothpaste to feminine hygiene products); buy household cleaning products; pay for repairs and for the replacement of dishes, glassware, furniture, bedding, and basic appliances; and buy myriad other items ranging from school supplies and a few presents to postage stamps and newspapers. Suppose that all of these expenditures, taken together, came to around $3,500 over the year. Adding in federal income, Social Security taxes, and state income taxes of $3,270, the total budget of such a family in 1994 would have required just about

$24,600. The American public's estimate of the smallest amount of income needed in 1994 for a family of four just to get by would be right on target.[16]

Even at nearly $25,000, the budget includes no money for entertainment; there is nothing budgeted for a vacation; no money is included for child care or for lessons or any summer activities or other experiences for the children; nothing for emergencies—say, were illness to result in any loss of pay due to absence from work—or for any savings to help pay for college for the children or to help an aging parent or to meet unexpected medical or other expenses; no money even for haircuts. The budget approximates the smallest income realistically capable of supporting a minimal mainstream standard of living.

In 1955 the average American family spent one third, or 33 percent, of its budget on food and the federal poverty-line formula started from the cost of the economy food plan and multiplied that cost by three. In 1994 the average family spent about 17.6 percent of its income on food and the annual cost of the United States Department of Agriculture's economy food budget for a four-person family was $4,576. By the actual original formula, then, the official poverty line in 1994 for such a family should have come to almost $26,000. Instead, the official poverty line reported by the government, at about $15,000 for 1994, was calculated by going back to the same budget for a 1955 standard of living and simply expressing that budget in 1994 dollars.

Both the Gallup and Roper survey findings and the true poverty-line formula itself corroborate what the itemized family budget shows; it required a base-line income of approximately $25,000 in 1994 for a family of four, realistically, to be able to reach the minimum level of a mainstream standard of living.[17]

As households fall beneath this level of income (adjusted to the size of the household), they begin to run short on the basics.[18] They juggle bills on a regular basis and make late payments. They increasingly have to rely on others for assistance— to cover repair bills, to pay for food, to get school clothes for their children. They know that one terror or another lies just ahead; a child with a high fever means a horrifying decision about whether to spend money on a doctor. They may agonize for days over whether to get a few simple decorations to make a birthday special or whether to spend a couple of dollars on a bottle of aspirin. They sometimes will need to go to great lengths to make ends meet, using cardboard to repair children's worn shoes rather than buying new or used ones, keeping the heat below 60 degrees in winter, or moving to a deteriorating and unsafe neighborhood. When money starts running out, car insurance often will be among the first things to go, with the result that many of these families have no insurance. Lack of insurance may lead to the car's impoundment, or poor repair to the car's incapacitation, which is likely to be old and run-down in any case. Either way, the car sits idle until the money can be borrowed or somehow cobbled together to pay off the impoundment or to fix it. For families living beneath this basic income, it's a bitter struggle, an everyday squeeze: more than half of these families report that they do not have enough money at some point during the year for food, clothing, or medical care.[19]

Yet if it takes a family of two adults and two children somewhere near $25,000 a year to reach the mainstream, such families also contain more than one worker capable of bringing in this income. During the time of the American Revolution, both husband and wife contributed to the economic foundation and material well-being of the household,[20] just as is common in the cases of most households today. Yet the contribution of each partner today comes principally in the form of paid employment outside the home, while in Revolutionary times it customarily involved work carried on either inside the home or on the household's property, which fit in relatively comfortably with the care, raising, and protection of children. This no longer holds true today for most households.

As a result, parents today need to take into account the financial costs of child care as well as its psychological effects on the children and themselves; many choose to have (and most would like the option of having) one partner work part-time rather than full-time.[21] Fewer than half of all married households containing children have two year-round full-time workers in the labor market. Considering the expense of day care, there indeed is little or no practical economic advantage in the cases of households earning low wages for the second earner to work more than three-quarters time.[22]

A part-time second earner will likely earn 85 percent or less of the prime earner's hourly wage.[23] Working three-quarters time, he or she would earn about 65 percent of the total wage of the primary earner.[24] To end up with the $25,000 base-line income called for in 1994, the secondary earner would have to bring in almost $10,000 and the primary earner would have to provide just over $15,000. For a wage to reach just over $15,000, or more, the prime earner would have to occupy a job paying at least about $7.60 per hour, or more, and the job would have to offer year-round full-time work (forty hours a week, fifty-two weeks a year except for legal public holidays), amounting to two thousand hours during the year. This total earnings and hourly wage level or better, in 1994, is what I call an adequate or mainstream job.[25] Attaining independence through such a job entails as many or more hours of work than generally were required of a person of common skill at the nation's founding.[26]

Quite apart from prime earners in households with four persons, a wide variety of other households are likely to view this earning level as the bottom line for a job. Consider, for example, a single-parent household with children. These households contain only a single earner and so have only one income. Indeed, in the cases of many single-parent households, a year-round full-time job at a base-line wage of $7.60 per hour and $15,200 for the year would be sufficient only if accompanied by at least average child-support payments from the absent parent.[27] In most locales, even households containing just a single individual needed close to $15,000 in 1994 in order to attain a mainstream living standard on a budget without allowances for entertainment or vacation, emergencies or saving.[28]

To be able to make it into the mainstream, virtually every kind of household requires at least one such job.[29] Coupled with the amount of house-related work that today's prime earner ordinarily carries out, the total time devoted to employment and maintenance of the household would amount to about fifty-three hours weekly, or about nine hours a day each of six days a week over the whole year, this not including the time consumed by getting to and from work.[30]

During the 1950s the base-line wage needed for households to reach the outer edge of the mainstream was quite similar to the minimum wage. Based on the public's response to polls in 1950 about the smallest family income required to get along, the base-line wage for that year would have been 76 cents an hour; the federal minimum wage for the same year was 75 cents. Over the following twenty-eight years, from 1950 to 1978, Congress made a series of adjustments to the minimum wage. These adjustments succeeded in raising the minimum wage, each time, to a level that was no less than 84 percent of the base-line wage for the respective year (see Table 2). Only following 1978 was the minimum wage, even after being adjusted, permitted to drop beneath 80 percent of the base-line wage. By 1989 the minimum wage had fallen to 55 percent of the base-line wage. Numerous observers have advanced the argument that the decline in the minimum wage relative to what it takes to attain a mainstream standard of living is compelling testimony to the erosion of economic opportunity. Yet this is not necessarily so. The level of the minimum wage relative to the cost of living says little about the number of decent-paying jobs that exist in the economy or whether there are enough of these jobs for the number of households needing them. The availability of a large number of adequate jobs—year-round full-time work paying at least a base-line wage or better—is perfectly compatible with a low minimum wage or, possibly, with no minimum wage at all.

Table 2.

MINIMUM WAGE AND BASE-LINE WAGE, 1950 AND 1989, AND FOR SELECTED YEARS WHEN MINIMUM WAGE WAS INCREASED

	Minimum Wage	Base-line Wage	Minimum Wage as a Percentage of Base-line Wage
1950	.75	.76	99
1956	1.00	1.11	90
1963	1.25	1.33	94
1967	1.40	1.59	88
1974	2.00	2.39	84
1978	2.65	3.17	84
1981	3.35	4.36	77
1989	3.35	6.10	55

Are there enough adequate jobs? The number of jobs available in the economy at any one point in time includes more than the number that workers actually occupy. The economy at each moment contains vacant jobs, some of which are never filled. Those never-filled jobs, sometimes called "depressed jobs," represent opportunities and ought not to be overlooked or ignored. Also, opportunities exist in the economy for workers to be enterprising. They can start their own businesses and attain decent livelihoods by becoming self-employed, so it is essential in calculating the number of adequate jobs available in the economy to include estimates of never-filled or "depressed" vacancies as well as opportunities for self-employment (see Appendix A).[31]

On the other side of the equation there are a number of households that do not need adequate jobs because they do not primarily support themselves through employment. These households include most of the elderly (who depend upon Social Security or private pension benefits), the early retired (who depend upon savings and private pension benefits), and households headed by persons who are disabled and supported by disability assistance. The remaining households either do or are expected to support themselves through employment.[32]

Yet simply having the same number of adequate jobs as there are households dependent upon employment will not suffice. This is because a free market operates in terms of individuals, not households, and adequate jobs in a free market can be taken by any individual. As a result, some households can and do occupy more than one adequate job without regard to whether there is a satisfactory supply of adequate jobs left for the remaining households.

Not every American has considered it good policy to allow households the freedom to occupy two or more adequate jobs. When, in an attempt to give every worker a living wage, Henry

Ford in 1914 *doubled* the minimum wage of his workers to 65 cents an hour, it was an extraordinary action. At the same time, since it was a living wage, he also undertook to deny work to married women with employable husbands, and hired private investigators "to visit workers' homes and ensure compliance."[33] Theoretically, the private market could follow Ford's lead in limiting each household to a single job, but Ford's approach depended upon his view of married women as subsidiaries. At the time, they were in numerous respects the legal property of their husbands. Not many people advocate going back to those days. Women are citizens in the full sense of the term today. Few would be prepared to urge that either business collusion or legislation place restrictions on the freedom of women as citizens to enter and leave the labor market.

The underlying question, then, is this: Do enough filled and unfilled adequate jobs exist to meet the need of every household expected to support itself through employment, taking into consideration that any household, in a free market, may hold down more than one such job? Is economic opportunity available to all citizens sufficient for them to earn at least a minimally respectable living, enough of a living to give them a solid stake in the community, enough to underpin the virtues of work and perseverance, enough to enable them to take control of their own lives? Such opportunity was the underlying condition that the founders of the nation believed essential to a safe and a secure society and to the well-being of a free republic. Nothing less would be compatible with the proposition that declared the nation's birth. Nothing less would be compatible with the American Dream.

Chapter 5

THE OPPORTUNITY DEFICIT

"**G**o west young man," Horace Greeley advised fellow Americans in the mid-nineteenth century. Prior to the early twentieth century, the American frontier promised fertile land and an abundance of opportunity to homesteaders. Even after the Great Depression, during the 1940s and 1950s and 1960s, economic growth soared and seemingly offered plenty of good jobs and widespread economic opportunity to households willing to work to gain independence and move ahead.

Except during the Great Depression, concern about the availability of jobs to make a decent living kept in abeyance until the early 1970s. Even in the days of the New Frontier and the Great Society, when issues of education, job training, and equal opportunity and their effects on poverty came to the center of attention, most policy makers presumed that good jobs existed or would soon exist for decently educated, well-trained, and fairly treated workers. But without a gauge of such opportunity to provide an accurate measure, judgments about whether the nation's founding ethos did endure as a reality in the lives of its citizens remained little more than speculation.

Recently, worry has grown that the economy may have lost the capacity to generate sustained supplies of well-paying jobs. Corporate rightsizing, downsizing, and streamlining have raised a series of sobering questions. Numerous good jobs in our manufacturing industries vanished during the past two decades, ever since the early 1970s. Many people place responsibility on the increasing competitiveness of the global economy and the strangehold that the expanding tax and regulatory burdens of government have put on American companies, forcing businesses to cut their costs; they have done so partly through automation coupled with the creation of low-paying jobs, whether full-time, part-time, or temporary. "Robots with flesh," is the way one person depicted America's growing army of temps. Many millions of poor, low-paying jobs have come into being in these past twenty years.

So, too, have a great number of adequate jobs—year-round full-time jobs paying base-line wages or better (at least $7.60 per hour, or more, in 1994). Consider the fifteen years from 1974 to 1989, which lie at the heart of the period of time during which people's doubts grew. The economy added nearly 15 million of these jobs, a leap of about 30 percent, in the space of those years.[1] During the same period, the nation's population rose by about half that: by 16 percent. Looking at the situation at the end of those years, in 1989, enables us to knife through the confusion by letting us examine the balance between opportunity and need after a lengthy period when the economy had been operating at high speed. In 1989, the nation concluded its seventh straight year of continuous economic growth without a recession, a new peace-time record. The recovery, which began in the last month of 1982, did not end until the late summer of 1990. During 1984 the economy experienced 6.2 percent real growth, the best single year since 1951, when the Korean War aided production. More than 9 million adequate jobs were created during the years from 1983 to 1990. In 1989 unemployment declined to 5.2 percent, a level many economists considered nearly the equivalent of full employment, the best the economy could do without creating the risk of an inflationary spiral. The annual rate of joblessness has not fallen below a level of 5 percent since then. The bellwether of the New York Stock Exchange, the Dow Jones, *tripled* during the period. By a host of standards, the poignant presidential campaign advertisements declaring it to be "morning in America," the signal theme of the victorious Reagan reelection campaign, had powerful evidence to back them up. At the 100th meeting of the American Economics Association in late 1987, incoming president and Nobel laureate Gary Becker concluded his address by saying, "Family welfare is the principal goal of a well-run economic system."[2] Given the vigorous economic growth of the 1980s, one would expect that families willing to work hard should have had little difficulty making their way.

That was not the case, however, despite the apparent good times, sustained over many years. Too few jobs existed by far for the number of households needing them. In 1989 there were 66.5 million households dependent upon employment for a living, excluding the households with retired or disabled heads,[3] but there were only 61.7 million adequate jobs.[4] The gap of 4.8 million jobs amounted to an absolute deficit relative to the total number of households dependent upon employment. Moreover, the 61.7 million adequate jobs could accommodate only 50.8 million households, because 10.9 million households occupied more than one adequate job. Altogether, 15.7 million house-holds were left out. No matter how hard they searched, there would not be enough adequate jobs. Consider that this shortage refers to deficiencies in the kinds of jobs required for households to reach merely the outermost fringes of a mainstream lifestyle after incorporating the pay of a second earner, and then only after further assuming that double the number of households proved able to succeed than actually did by way of creating their own jobs and that every available job on offer got filled. Even had the heads of the 15.7 million excluded households been suf-ficiently competitive as to have gotten half the jobs held by sec-ond earners,[5] the deficit would still have amounted to greater than 10 million adequate jobs in 1989.[6] Such a large shortfall might be understandable in a time of recession, but this was at the top of the nation's longest continuous peacetime recovery, after millions of new adequate jobs had been created.

There are several considerations that might modify this disturbing picture. Some say the availability of jobs in the econ-omy depends mostly on the availability of willing workers: if idle and unemployed people are averse to work, employers have little incentive to create new jobs. Yet the evidence suggests that this consideration had no more than a modest influence. Many of the household heads without an adequate job were far from idle. They worked. About 7 million heads of households, in fact, worked year-round full-time and were fully employed in jobs paying less than the base-line wage. Economic theory would argue that the economy could not have added many more jobs in any case. The unemployment rate for 1989, at 5.2 percent, is considered by many economists to be close to full employment.[7] This means that in the eyes of these economists, not too many more jobs could have been created by the economy, or new work-ers hired, without producing a spiral of inflation culminating in the destabilization of the economy. The economy had already absorbed nearly all the workers it safely could.

Some households are headed by the young or by the undereducated, and one might interpret the American ethos as saying that neither youth nor the undereducated should have an expectation of immediate economic independence, that youth might have to put in six or seven sustained years of work before moving to independence, and that the undereducated should first complete the customary basic education, which in 1989 would have required earning at least a high school diploma.[8] Suppose, then, that we exclude all households headed by young persons under age twenty-five or by persons without a high school diploma[9] and the jobs they occupy from the picture. In 1989 that would have left 53.4 million households (headed by persons of at least age twenty-five with a high school diploma or postsecondary education) competing for 44.6 million adequate jobs, still resulting in a shortfall of nearly 9 million adequate jobs.

Based on the belief that steady work coupled with education will bring success, it is commonly thought that low-paid jobs are occupied mostly by the undereducated, especially by high school dropouts. This is a mistake. Even during the record seventh consecutive year of economic growth, in 1989, more than two thirds of all workers employed in year-round full-time jobs paying less than the base-line wage had graduated from high school,[10] and more than a third had completed at least some postsecondary education. In fact, a larger number of workers occupying these jobs had at least some post secondary education or a college degree than were high school dropouts. Of all male workers aged twenty-five and above, with above-average achievement motivation[11] and some postsecondary education, about one in twelve working year-round full-time in 1989 nevertheless held jobs paying less than the base-line wage. Still more of these workers, unable to find full-time work, occupied low-paying part-time jobs or were unemployed. "People who had years of college can't find anything," Nancy Muse, a resident of Northridge, California, told *The New York Times*.[12] According to the Bureau of Labor Statistics' estimates, nearly 25 percent of all employed college graduates were working at jobs that did not require a degree.

The implication is clear. Jobs paying low wages were not simply the result of subpar educational credentials among workers or insufficient ambition. A gross deficit of 15.7 million jobs when there are 66.5 million households amounts to an overall gap of 23.6 percent, nearly *five* times the unemployment rate for 1989 of 5.2 percent. When a shortage of adequate jobs exists on this scale, a tremendous crowding occurs. Even people with above-average educational credentials and above-average ambition will be forced, in surprising numbers, to take jobs that fail to bring them into the societal mainstream.

And many workers in low-paying jobs will be unable to move up. Of married male heads of household having two or more children, who were employed in year-round full-time jobs paying less than the base-line wage in 1979, 56 percent still occupied inadequate jobs and another 5.7 percent were unemployed ten years later.[13] This remained just as true if the household head had finished high school or had some postsecondary education.[14] Moreover, those workers who remained in inadequate jobs were joined by nearly one in nine of their peers who had been fortunate enough to hold adequate jobs in 1979. Few were exempt from downward mobility, not even graduates of Harvard.[15]

Discipline and perseverance—working year after year without pause—did not improve matters by much, either. Even if they were employed year-round full-time all ten years, consecutively, 66 percent of the heads of household occupying inadequate jobs in 1979 ended the decade in 1989 still earning less than a base-line wage, just as they had begun. For these many households, long years of work simply did not pay off. Once again, having a high school degree or some postsecondary education made little difference.[16]

The fact that a substantial shortage of opportunity existed closing out millions of workers did not mean that no one at all was able to get ahead. The 1980s and 1990s produced many anecdotal examples of Americans lifting themselves up by their bootstraps and ending solidly within the respectable mainstream in Horatio Alger style or indeed rising all the way from rags to riches. Take the experience of David and Wanda Lloyd of Sheboygan, Wisconsin.[17] In 1989 the Lloyds had been reduced to homelessness and were surviving on food stamps. Both David and Wanda had lost their jobs due to the closure of the woodworking factory where they were employed. They were forced to live in their car with their two children. As members of the "new poor," they could not have descended lower in their own eyes. To avoid being seen using food stamps, they shopped at night when fewer people were around. The pain was overwhelming, but both of them ultimately found good jobs again. Four years after David had gotten his new job, he had been promoted three times and, working long hours, had risen to a wage of $36,000 a year. Their transformation of defeat into victory through hard work and perseverance exemplifies the American success story.

Consider, also, Warren Anderson's story. He began working for minimum wage at a Jack-in-the-Box in San Clemente, California, in 1980, when he was seventeen years old. By 1994 he had been promoted to shift leader, assistant manager, and then manager of a $1.5 million business on his way to becoming supervisor of several restaurants, earning a salary with bonuses totaling more than $50,000 yearly at just thirty-one years of age.[18] There are stunning rags-to-riches examples, too, such as that of the comedian Jim Carrey. When Carrey was a teenager, his father became jobless, eventually costing his family their home. They were forced to set up house in a tent on Carrey's older sister's front lawn.[19] Only a few years later, however, Carrey was earning $200,000 a year and would soon command contracts in the millions of dollars for his comedic roles in films. The inspiring examples of David and Wanda Lloyd, Warren Anderson, Jim Carrey, or of Clarence Thomas, from Pinpoint, Georgia, and Colin Powell, from New York's South Bronx, have multiplied many times over, of course. America remains a land of tremendous opportunity when seen from this vantage point.

All the same, for every example of upward mobility there exists a compelling opposite story.[20] Jim and Nancy Cash, who live near St. Louis, each have two years of community college education beyond high school. In their late thirties with two children, they earn $21,600 combined, he working full-time as a house and sign painter, she working nearly full-time as a clerk at a discount store. He's attempted four different occupations over the last twenty years, including trying to start his own business. He's been employed full-time in his present job for nearly six years. Describing their prospects for the future, Jim said, the light in his eyes seeming almost extinguished, "It feels like you're pinned to the ground. I've worked forty or fifty hours a week and more, do good work, and can't get past getting nothin'. We have to beg from friends and relatives to make it, scrounge from the food bank. I hunt through Dumpsters and behind stores. It's degrading. I feel humiliated." Stanley and Rachael Yanovich are in their early forties with three children, the oldest of whom is about to graduate from high school. He works as a full-time security guard and she as a data processor; together they earn less than $21,000. Their only car has been out of commission for five months. They can't afford to get it fixed and have no money for the insurance on it either. "Sometimes I cry myself to sleep," Rachael told me. There is Rebecca Blackwell, aged thirty-six with two children—one seven and the other ten years old—who earned a degree at a technical school after completing high school. Employed as a nurse's aide, she earns $12,700 yearly and receives about $2,500 a year from the children's father. She has given up a telephone and is two months behind on both the rent and the electricity. She has nightmares of ending up a bag lady on the streets. Ernst and Anna Bartelle are both in their fifties. She manages the office of a social service agency and he is a maintenance worker for a high school. Their joint income of $21,900 allows them and their two children so little that "sometimes we've gone days just eating potatoes and eggs . . . sometimes just potatoes." Describing her life, Anna said, "You ever seen a hamster in a cage? It just runs and runs on its wheel and gets nowhere. That's what I feel like sometimes." Like the stories of the upwardly mobile, the examples of the Bartelles, the Blackwells, the Yanoviches, and the Cashes have multiplied many times over, too.

Indeed, massive numbers of Americans share them, as we have seen. Skeptics may claim that these men and women, of every race and level of education, could and should have tried still harder than they did. Their willpower and effort are not the real issue, though. They encountered a severe shortage of opportunity, totaling in the millions of adequate jobs, even assuming a doubling of the growth of successful entrepreneurship and self-employment. Given the scarcity of opportunity, steady full-time work sustained over many years, coupled with a decent level of education, is not necessarily enough in this country to enable people managing frugally to attain a mainstream standard of living. Some workers who are poor will make it, of course. A substantial shortage of adequate jobs does not mean that no opportunity exists at all, that no one will have winning entrepreneurial ideas along with the level of energy, aptitude, personality, access to resources, and good luck required to advance them over time to success, or will find job openings enabling them to rise from poverty to independence. It does mean that many millions of responsible and hardworking people will not be so fortunate.

Some say that the American Dream is meant to be realized not by the present generation of adults but by their children. A family may have to start in a wind-chilled flat, and the heat often may be out of order, but the hope for the parents is that through their hard work and perseverance their children will one day be able to live the good life. Still, even in immigrant families, while the parents' point of reference may be memories of the conditions they left in their former homelands, the reference point of the native-born is here at home. Once the next generation has reached adulthood, hope for this second generation must ultimately turn into reasonable expectation for the *present* generation. At some point, the American Dream must refer not simply to a future generation but to the generation here and now.

The immigrant story is itself full of fascinating complexities, of course. Fabled examples of immigrant families who come here with nothing, with barely any knowledge of the language, and ultimately rise into the middle class or achieve wealth give credence to the ideal of America as the land of opportunity. The fact that hundreds of thousands of first-generation immigrants have found prosperity in America within a relatively short time raises the question "If they can do it, why can't the native-born?" It sometimes goes unmentioned that groups of first-generation immigrants typically lauded for their success in this country often have a higher level of education than do the native-born.

For example, the average education of first-generation male immigrants to the United States from Japan, Korea, and Vietnam as of 1980 was in each case higher than for native-born males—in the instance of Japan, nearly three years higher.[21] Despite this, the poverty rates among immigrants from each of these countries (and the overall poverty rate among all immigrant families) was higher than among the native-born.[22] Even twenty to thirty years after entry into the United States, immigrant families—both male- and female-headed—have somewhat higher rates of welfare assistance than do native-born families.[23]

For both the native-born and the immigrant, the overriding issue is whether economic opportunity is plentiful or limited. In 1989 an immense deficit of adequate jobs existed. But is this situation new? The previous comparable year, also at the height of a business cycle, was 1979. The earliest year for which appropriate data exist was 1967,[24] itself seven years into the life of the business cycle that began in 1960.

In 1967 45.8 million households had to make their living through an economy in which 42.0 million adequate jobs were available in all. Moreover, about 5.1 million of the available jobs were taken by supplemental earners in households holding more than one such job, which left 36.9 million of these jobs to cover 45.8 million households—a gap of 8.9 million adequate jobs, or a 19.4 percent shortfall. The unemployment rate for the year, by contrast, stood at 3.7 percent.

The exceedingly low unemployment figures for the mid-1960s make the period appear to many observers to have been a golden age of opportunity. All the same, a large number of families were left out, a fact that youth soon to enter the world of employment understood at the time. A considerable number of them expressed concern about whether they would be able to get decent work. In the midst of the Kennedy–Johnson years, an in-depth survey of secondary school children in Richmond, California, found that 29.9 percent of black male youths and 19.5 percent of nonblack male youths were very worried about being able to find a job after they got out of school;[25] moreover, 21.4 percent of the black males and 17.2 percent of nonblack males believed that the absence of jobs would keep them from getting the kind of job they eventually wanted.[26] Given these perceptions, it is no surprise that a sizable number of them—26.5 percent of the black males and 28.1 percent of their non-black peers—believed that opportunities for success were not available to everyone.[27]

There are indications that the shortfall in adequate jobs perceived by youth in the mid-1960s grew worse over the prior ten to fifteen years, since the first half of the 1950s. While the precise data needed to measure the total hours and wage levels of all year-round full-time workers do not exist going back into the 1950s,[28] data do show that many fewer jobs came into being from 1950 to 1965 than the number of new households (11.2 million net new jobs from 1950 to 1965 were created, both ade-quate and otherwise, as compared with the formation of 13.1 million new nonelderly households). Moreover, increasing num-bers of jobs during the period were taken by female spouses from households in which the husband was also employed full-time. The number of second earners grew from about 8.6 million in 1950 to about 14.7 million in 1965.[29] Thus, in 1965 there not only were 2 million more new households than new jobs but 6 million more second earners than in 1950. It is plausible that the job shortage facing households in the latter 1960s had been growing over the prior fifteen years.

The job shortage that existed in 1967 was never eliminat-ed. The situation changed direction and moderated during the

1970s, in the business cycle that reached its apogee in 1979. In that year, 56.0 million adequate jobs existed for the 56.2 million households needing them. This virtual match between the number of adequate jobs and households, however, doesn't consider the households holding more than one adequate job. In 1979 about 8.1 million of the adequate jobs were held by supplemental earners in households with two or more such jobs, leaving a reduced although still sizable shortfall of 8.3 million jobs, a 14.8 percent gap.

From that point forward, the basic level of economic opportunity available to American households experienced a stunning deterioration, resulting in a total shortage of more than 15 million jobs by 1989. It seemed to appear out of nowhere. But then again, the magnitude of the shortage of opportunity had been well concealed, over the entire period, by the official measures the government used to gauge the economic well-being of American households. A chief culprit was the unemployment rate. Unemployment statistics receive considerable public attention every month and are taken as one of the best indicators of whether economic opportunity is in reasonable or short supply. Yet the unemployment rate gave no hint of the scarcity of adequate opportunity facing Americans over the period (see Sidebar). A decline (rise) in unemployment did not correspond with a reduced (increased) scarcity of adequate opportunity. More important, the unemployment rate always remained far below the true job deficit, by an order of magnitude of two to five or more times. Official statistics sorely misled the nation about the shortfall of opportunity that existed and its level of seriousness as well as its direction of change. It's hard to conceive of a better recipe for the creation of public misunderstanding, or the incapacitation of public policy, or the development of popular alienation and frustration.

Sidebar

RATES OF UNEMPLOYMENT AND SCARCITY OF ADEQUATE OPPORTUNITY, 1967, 1979, AND 1989.

	1967	1979	1989
Rate of Unemployment	3.7	5.8	5.2
Rate of Scarcity of Adequate Jobs	19.4	14.8	23.6

The perception that opportunity was widely available in the 1980s fueled the politics of the day and undergirded beliefs that other causes—not lack of opportunity—lay at the root of low incomes and economic disadvantage. Voicing the opinion of many others, David Frum of *The Wall Street Journal* concluded in 1994 that a scarcity of opportunity had very little to do with either the economic problems facing the poor during the 1980s or the spread of social pathologies often associated with low income. "There had been opportunities galore in the 1980's," he wrote.[30] Low rates of unemployment that stood at the full-employment level of 5 percent, coupled with strong levels of job creation and economic growth year after year, made it seem as if the 1980s had radiated with opportunity. The surface appearances upon which such beliefs were formed and subsequent analyses were constructed, though, stood light-years away from the grim reality that millions of American families actually faced in their daily lives.

No less mistaken are many of the popular explanations for the sharp upward leap in the job shortage that took place during the 1980s. Numerous observers fault the economy's performance, alleging that the economy suffered from the cumulating burdens of governmental intrusions over past years and from the increasingly intense competition for global markets.[31] Yet the economy grew at a speed not dramatically different from the growth rate that the British economy achieved at the height of the industrial revolution.[32] It generated more than 7 million net new adequate jobs between 1979 and 1989[33] (indeed, it added more than 9 million such jobs from 1983 to 1989, following job losses during the 1980–82 recession). Seven million adequate jobs in a decade equals the *total* new job creation (including part-time and low-paying full-time jobs) in Germany, France, Great Britain, and Italy combined, with a population similar to the United States, over the span of *two* decades from 1970 to 1990.[34] It surpasses the total new job creation managed by the American economy during the halcyon decade of the 1950s. Nonetheless, following 1979, adequate jobs capable of lifting households into the mainstream became increasingly scarce *relative to the number of households needing them in combination with the additional second earners and earners who were competing for them.* This shortage can be attributed to changing demographic patterns far more than to a poor performance by the economy. The demographic forces were overwhelming. They included the newly formed households of the gigantic baby boomer generation along with the change in cultural norms regarding gender roles and employment. From 1979 to 1989 increased demand for adequate jobs resulted from a 10.3 million rise in new nonelderly households dependent upon the economy, coupled with the addition of 2.7 million new supplemental earners and about 1.6 million unrelated individu-als[35] occupying adequate jobs. These trends combined added more than 14 million in demand, dwarfing the creation of net new adequate jobs by the economy. Nearly the entire growth in households from 1979 to 1989, above and beyond normal growth, arose from the larger number of adults contained in the baby boom generation.[36]

The impact of the baby boom generation was not exclusive to the 1980s, of course, but influenced the formation of households during the 1970s and late 1960s as well. The job deficit stabilized in the years from 1967 to 1979 largely because an extraordinary performance by the nation's economy produced new adequate jobs at a rate surpassing an average 1.2 million each year, exceeding 2 percent yearly, over a period that included the steep recession of 1973–75. No economy could be expected to create new adequate jobs at this pace for an indefinite period. It is seemingly beyond the capabilities demonstrated by any industrial nation during the past three decades.[37]

Given the relevance of demographic trends to the creation of the shortfall in opportunity, might a reversal of these trends, as the baby boom generation's entry into the workforce is followed by that of a generation significantly smaller in size, correct the situation? Tempering such a prospect is the possibility that the job situation grew worse over the 1950s and early 1960s, leaving a 19 percent gap by 1967, *prior* to the baby boom generation's massive entry into the labor market. There is no iron law by which the economy's production of jobs, or of adequate jobs, necessarily keeps pace with the normal rate of household formation, let alone surpasses that rate in order to close an existing deficit of jobs.

A more important consideration, though, is the sheer size of the shortfall. A deficit of 15 million (or even 10 million) adequate jobs, leaving out 23 percent of all households, is immense. Fewer than two out of every three jobs created over the past three decades have been adequate jobs (the remainder were part-time jobs or low-paying full-time jobs). Moreover, at normal levels now each year a net addition of about 900,000 new households needing employment occurs and another 200,000 additional second earners take adequate jobs. The creation of about 1.8 million net new jobs (included among them 1.1 million adequate jobs) will be necessary just to absorb them. As a result, if a strong economy were to generate 2.6 million new jobs on average each and every year[38] (producing a surplus of 800,000 jobs a year, among them 500,000 adequate jobs), it would take three full decades at this level of job creation, with no slowdown or recession, for the economy to deliver the needed 15 million adequate jobs.[39] The American Dream—the set of beliefs that links our aspirations today with the precepts of the nation at its birth—not only is an impossibility now for millions of households around the nation, but no reasonable level of job creation by the economy, no matter how well sustained into the foreseeable future, will be able to close the breach.

POSTSCRIPT

Calculating that it requires the creation of around 1.8 million net new jobs a year in order to stay even with the increased need for adequate jobs from new households and supplemental earners (see pages 86–87), it is possible to estimate where the nation's opportunity deficit stood at the end of 1996. Following 1989, a poor performance in job creation occurred for three years through 1992. During those three years, barely 1 million net new jobs came into being. Thereafter, an excellent performance from 1993 through 1996 led to the creation of 10 million new jobs thereafter, resulting in the overall addition of 11 million net new jobs over the seven years from 1989 to 1996, or 1.6 million per year for the period. This amounts to slightly less than the 1.8 million added jobs a year necessary to keep abreast of new demand for adequate jobs. Despite the economy's stellar performance in job growth between 1993 and 1996, it is likely that the 15.7 million deficit in adequate jobs existing in 1989 did not close by the end of 1996 but remained approximately at that same level.

Chapter

6

WORK, WAGES, AND THE PROGRESS OF THE TYPICAL AMERICAN FAMILY

The existence of minimally adequate employment opportunities capable of lifting households into the mainstream represents one element of the American ethos. A second vital element concerns the capacity of typical American households, even if already within the mainstream, to be able to advance their standard of living through improved performance. During the past two decades, however, serious questions have arisen about how much truth still exists in the maxim that the average American family has the ability to get ahead. Since 1973 production workers, who comprise three quarters of the entire workforce, have seen their real wage levels not merely stagnate but actually decline by 13 percent. From 1955 to 1973, by contrast, the real wages of the nation's production workers climbed by about 38 percent, an advance of about 2 percent a year.[1] For all workers, average real wages fell by 8 percent from 1979 to 1994.

Use of evidence about the average wage of workers is quite common, but such wage comparisons over time do not confine themselves to the same workers. Production workers (or all workers), taken as a group, may contain a higher proportion of young and inexperienced workers at one point in time than at another. The increase (or decrease) in the average wage might be entirely or partly an artifact of such differences. What we want to know, with respect to questions about mobility or advancement, is what happened to the same workers from one year to another.

Looking at the same workers over time to see how the fortunes of the median such worker changed from one year to another,[2] we find that 57.2 percent of heads of household who worked year-round full-time, both in 1979 and in 1989, experienced a real gain in hourly pay. The median such gain was about 11 percent over those ten years, or about 1 percent a year. Of heads of household employed at least half-time in both years,[3] 57.3 percent succeeded in attaining a real gain in hourly pay, with a median advance (once more) of about 11 percent. A similar result occurs again if we compare all workers who were employed for at least four weeks in both 1979 and 1989. It appears, then, that a slim majority of household heads who were working got a real increase in pay.

Even so, the struggle had become increasingly fierce. Many household heads were finding it far more difficult to get ahead than had been the case in earlier years, when a greater proportion of workers received real increases, and the increases were sharply higher ones. From 1967 to 1973 nearly 75 percent of working heads of household experienced a real increase in pay, with a median gain of 3.1 percent a year. On the other hand, after 1973 the advance in real pay slowed down considerably to 1 percent from the earlier 3 percent, and the pay of about 42 percent of household heads actually declined. In addition, whether they had managed to get pay raises or not, millions of workers occupied jobs paying so poorly as to strand them outside the margins of a mainstream living standard. By 1989, in fact, *half* of all household heads who worked full-time that year and were employed in 1979 either still worked for less than an adequate wage or sustained a real decline in their wage during the decade. Economic pain now reached the average American household.

Signs suggest that these trends did not end with the 1980s but persisted in the 1990s. Through December 1995 a series of polls indicate that more Americans perceived that their incomes were falling behind the cost of living than felt their incomes were moving ahead.[4] As indicated earlier, the massive deficit in adequate jobs remained much the same from 1989 to 1996 as well.[5]

Why did the struggle of American workers grow so onerous during the years following the early 1970s? Neither the level of governmental spending, taxation, and regulation nor the increasing penetration of cutthroat global trade competition, though many observers suspect them, are chief players in an explanation.[6] Three general considerations of greater importance deserve to take center stage in the public's discussion. The first concerns the growth of wage inequality among workers; the second has to do with the widening gap between wage gains and gains in worker performance; and the third involves a slowdown in the overall rate of improved productivity of the American labor force. Any solution to combat the wage immobility confronting American families effectively will need to come to grips with these three factors.

One form of wage inequality has grown dramatically in the United States over the past two decades: the gulf separating the average worker (as well as low-paid workers) from the highest-paid workers. A growing maldistribution has occurred especially among males. In 1970 the top one fifth of all male workers earned twice the pay of the middle fifth of workers; less than two decades later, in 1986, the workers in the top fifth were receiving 2.4 times as much pay as the middle fifth received.[7] Had the wage distribution remained at the 1970 level, and pay increases in all earning classes risen in roughly similar proportion instead of going mostly to the top fifth, the average pay for the remaining workers would have advanced by nearly one third more—producing a wage gain of about 1.5 percent a year for the median worker instead of 1.1 percent.[8] Since each year's increase accumulates over time, by 1986 the average gain for the median year-round full-time male worker would have exceeded $1,300 a year, and by 1995 about $2,400 a year, or $1.20 an hour.

In addition, the compensation received by the whole work-force (now also adding in the earnings of the top fifth) failed to keep up with improvements in performance. Average productivity per hour among all workers climbed by more than one quarter from 1973 to 1994.[9] Yet the average real compensation of all workers per hour (including benefits) grew by only 9 percent,[10] a difference on average of about 0.8 per year.[11] Two effects were occurring simultaneously: first, the total level of compensation growth was depressed by about 0.8 percent on average each year relative to the productivity improvements that took place; second, rising wage inequality meant that any advances in total compensation that did occur over the period barely trickled down to the ordinary worker. Together they cost the average worker 1.2 percent in wage growth a year. Just 1 percent added wage growth a year over a two-decade period would have resulted in increased yearly earnings exceeding $5,000 for the median year-round full-time worker by 1995. The effect of any recent proposal aimed at reducing taxes to boost the after-tax income available to average families pales into obscurity by comparison.

One explanation often heard for the growing wage inequality and rising gap between productivity and compensation is that American workers were overpaid relative to rival workers in the global marketplace, and in order for them to regain a competitive position internationally, the workers' pay had to be reduced even while their productivity increased. However, global trade accounts for only a relatively small fraction of the overall economy (less than 15 percent).[12] Trade with low-wage nations accounts for less still (below 3 percent). Did we compare well with our major trading rivals, however? Even in areas like manufacturing, a sector where global trade is highly pertinent, by 1979 the wages of American workers were already competitive with those of key Western nations, such as Germany, whose industries proved highly successful in world markets; and the overall productivity of our manufacturing workers led the world and continues to be unsurpassed.[13] Despite wages in line with those of successful competitors and a real gain of 34 percent in productivity during the 1980s, however, America's manufacturing workers still failed to gain *any* real increase in wages over the entire decade. The relationship between improved productivity and wages, once considered inviolate, had disappeared. Moreover, if global competition were so decisive an influence, the salaries of the top fifth of American workers as compared with that of the average worker should not have fared so differently relative to what occurred among our major rival trading competitors, where the pay of the highest fifth of workers relative to the median worker is and has remained far lower than in the United States. While growing global competitiveness has made some difference, it has not likely been a decisive factor, certainly not by itself.[14]

A second explanation—one worth considering far more seriously than it has been to date—involves the change that has taken place in the power of labor over the past three decades. Whereas unions organized almost one in every three nonagricultural workers in 1970, that figure fell to 13 percent by 1992. As the bargaining strength of labor has declined, so have the wages of the median worker relative to those of the top fifth of workers as well as the wages of all workers relative to productivity improvements. A study of ten industrial nations from 1960 to 1990 reveals that the degree to which labor managed to maintain its strength exercised a significant influence on what factors ended up determining the growth of real wages. In nations where labor has remained strong, real wages were likely to be determined by factors such as improvements in worker productivity and efficiency. Where labor had grown weak, improvements in productivity and efficiency had little effect on the growth of wages, which was primarily determined by the size of the untapped labor pool available for work from domestic and international sources.[15] Governments could take the place of labor in developing policies that affect real wages so as to keep earnings abreast of productivity improvements, but governments, too, tend to be influenced by the extent to which labor is organized and powerful or weak and marginalized.

Still a third explanation also deserves attention. After 1968 the overall rate of improved productivity of the American workforce slowed down by more than half. As the baby boom generation poured into the labor force following the middle of the 1960s, the proportion of relatively young, new, and inexperienced workers making up the labor force rose considerably. For example, the proportion of the labor force over age forty-five increased from 34.3 to 38.1 percent between 1950 and 1965; by contrast, the proportion of these mature workers dropped from

38.1 to 29.8 percent from 1965 to 1992.[16] Young, new, and inexperienced workers are expected to be less productive than more senior and experienced workers. It is probable that the same set of workers who had been in the workforce before 1965 continued to improve their productivity at a pace somewhat closer to the rate experienced in the 1950s and early 1960s.

All the same, the falloff in productivity likely did have some effect on the performance of the more senior and experienced workers, as well, due partly to the very large number of new workers. The rate of expansion of the labor force doubled after 1965 as the total number of employed workers climbed from 71 million to 117 million, an increase of about 65 percent, with the result that the ratio of capital to labor declined. In addition, there was a sharp slowdown in the educational advancement of the workforce after 1970: from 1950 to 1970 the median years of education of the adult population had climbed one third from 9.3 to 12.1 years, while from 1970 to 1990 they rose by barely 5 percent—from 12.1 years to 12.7 years.[17] Surely this substantial slackening in educational advancement contributed to the declining growth of productivity and the slowdown in overall wage growth that took place over those years.[18]

The combination of the changed distribution in wages, the widening gulf separating productivity and compensation, and the lower growth in productivity itself, all coupled with the huge increase in the number of households, left an indelible mark. By the close of the 1980s, American households had faced a prolonged struggle against a shortage of economic opportunity which left millions of families feeling vulnerable and under enormous economic pressure, scrambling on a daily basis, their future no longer under their own control. These households had to confront a significant shortfall in basic opportunities to make a minimally decent livelihood—a shortage that abated slightly for a brief time during the 1970s before beginning to worsen dramatically in the 1980s, reaching beyond the 15 million mark. They also faced a dramatic slowdown in the improvement of the wages of the median American worker, so that another sizable and growing segment of workers who had attained the minimum found themselves unable to move ahead at all, with their wages stagnant or declining even if they held year-round full-time jobs and were steady and experienced workers. From 1973 to 1989, half of all fully employed household heads experienced either an actual reduction in pay over those sixteen years or found themselves unable to attain even a minimally adequate job, a condition that appears to have continued into the 1990s.[19] In this nation conceived in the values of independence and advancement based on the work ethic and on improved performance, is it any wonder that many millions of American households had become gravely fearful of the future?

POLITICAL AND

SOCIAL IMPLICATIONS

The nation's founders were both visionary idealists and pragmatic realists. As idealists, they envisioned a society constructed upon the economic independence and advancement of its citizens. They considered such a foundation essential to republican principles and, for many of them, to a society committed to a belief in the equal moral worth of human beings. Thomas Jefferson, to whom the Continental Congress turned for leadership, considered the concept of a society founded upon equal citizens who were economically independent to be so intrinsically right, so clearly vital to the good society, that he called the truth sacred and undeniable. This revolutionary idea—that all citizens should have the opportunity for a decent life and a decent livelihood—has given the nation a sense of moral direction and purpose ever since. Still inspiring American thinking two hundred years later, it continues to express what Americans believe to be among the nation's loftiest purposes.[1] To the degree that America does not live up to this ethos, it fails according to its own deepest sense of morality and basic system of values. This would be reason enough to take corrective action.

As pragmatists and realists, the Founding Fathers wrestled with issues of power and human psychology, of the capacity of society to remain well ordered and stable and the ability of government to function successfully. How could ordinarily selfish and self-serving human beings be brought to control themselves and to comply with a free—meaning uncoercive—republican government? The founders believed that the practical success of republican society and government would depend upon the level of respect for the individual rights of others that such a society could instill and maintain, which in turn would vitally depend upon economic conditions—particularly upon the opportunity for independence and advancement prevailing in the society.

Forty years ago, Americans had an abiding trust in their government. Today, fewer than one third of the populace does. Forty years ago, families generally went on welfare because the father was deceased or incapacitated. Today, illegitimacy and divorce are the overwhelmingly predominant reasons for welfare recipiency. Forty years ago, most Americans felt sufficiently protected and safe that they left their homes and cars unlocked. With the rise in rates of crime and juvenile delinquency, not many Americans feel that way any longer.

Changes such as these and many others like them have fundamentally altered the American landscape, creating the feeling that the nation's social and moral foundations have dangerously deteriorated and that the society may be fracturing. No single explanation, no one cause can account for these changes. Numerous forces, often interrelated, have been at play. Among the causes has been the existence of an environment of constricted economic opportunity and the feelings of despair and dismay it has generated. When cynicism sets in and affects large numbers of people, the persistence of its impact does not depend upon the precise level of the initial causal forces as much as on the continued manifestation of those forces over time at some level of significance. The general environment of constricted opportunity is as important as, if not more important than, the exact degree of shortage.

For most of our history the existence of the frontier muted issues about the availability of economic opportunity. There was a mythic belief that people facing hard times always had the option of picking up stakes and finding a decent life elsewhere. With respect to the contiguous forty-eight states, the nation didn't stop expanding until 1912, when both Arizona and New Mexico were admitted into statehood. Large tracts of land in the interior of the Northwest remained available to homesteaders, free, well into the 1920s. The tradition of "lighting out for the frontier" persisted for the next several decades thereafter in the form of waves of massive migrations out of the South and the poor rural hinterlands to urban centers all across the nation. From the 1950s on, however, to many who became entrenched in what were increasingly called inner-city "ghettos," the long-standing American answer of geographic mobility as a way for the economically disadvantaged to find untapped opportunity seemed ever less a realistic solution.

At the same time, societal developments during the 1950s and 1960s played a key role in influencing Americans' perceptions of the meaning and reality of independence and advancement. The civil rights movement, for instance, drew heavily on ideas about independence and opportunity, proclaiming that any individual who practiced the work ethic and persevered ought to be able to earn a minimally dignified living and move ahead, regardless of race or any artificial characteristic. Martin Luther King, Jr., famously asked that people be treated according to the content of their characters—their diligence, honesty, industriousness, and pride of work—rather than the color of their skin. If opportunity were plentiful, the implementation and effective enforcement of the civil rights agenda would enable all individuals of good character, from within the included and formerly excluded groups alike, to attain a respectable living and move ahead within the mainstream. In the words of Princeton University political scientist Jennifer Hochschild, "The ideology of equal opportunity [generated] hope and activity aimed at success in the social and economic mainstream."[2]

Just as these ideas accenting the equal right of access of all to a decent livelihood were gaining momentum, television entered people's homes, powerfully reinforcing the image of mainstream living standards in the minds of Americans. In 1950 scarcely 10 percent of American households had a television. By 1955 nearly 65 percent of households did. Five years later, in 1960, 90 percent had at least one, and the average household watched almost five hours of television each and every day. Prior to television, low-income Americans' first-hand familiarity with living standards other than their own might have been through personal acquaintances who lived nearby or in another neighborhood or another town. With the arrival of television, low-income households experienced absorbing images of middle-class lifestyles hour after hour every day, in the intimate surroundings of their own homes, while the right of equal access to the essential basis of this television-celebrated lifestyle acquired ever greater importance in the nation's consciousness.

The 1950s and 1960s brought America into a new and unprecedented era. The frontier as a potential alternate route of economic opportunity enabling hardworking poor people to advance had disappeared even as a lingering memory, while new-found societal developments like television and civil rights gave an enormous thrust to issues about the ability to attain a decent livelihood and economic advancement. Amid these powerful forces, the existence of a serious shortage of opportunity, mounting into many millions of jobs, had a multiplicity of implications.

For one, the shortage of opportunity amplified the challenges facing a number of major governmental programs, including those of the War on Poverty and the Great Society, ultimately dooming them to failure in the public's eyes. In President Johnson's view, the impoverished were disadvantaged. They were held back from entering the mainstream by poor education, housing, nutrition, and health care, coupled frequently, in the case of minorities, with discriminatory treatment. Given proper skills, a decent living environment, adequate health care, and fair treatment in the job and consumer markets, the President believed, the poor would be able to find opportunity enabling them to advance through the private economy. The Great Society and War on Poverty supported large-scale programs that assisted K–12 as well as postsecondary education, job training, nutrition, housing, and access to medical care along with civil rights to promote fair and equal treatment. A substantial portion of the effort was directed toward skills preparation and the removal of artificial barriers to employment and economic activity. It was, first and foremost, the philosophy of a "hand up instead of a handout." It depended on the unspoken assumption that skilled and healthy people, treated fairly, could become independent; that sufficient opportunity existed in the private economy, or would come to exist.

Yet in the mid-1960s *fewer* year-round full-time jobs actually existed, relative to the number of households dependent upon employment, than had been the case in 1950. By 1967 the shortfall in adequate opportunities as compared with the number of households stood at 19 percent, surpassing the year's unemployment rate by more than five times. The gap between the number of households needing adequate jobs and the availability of such jobs surpassed 8 million. Remember, this gap refers to a lack of the kinds of jobs required for households to reach merely the outermost fringes of a mainstream lifestyle, and even then only after assuming that these households got about two fifths of their earnings from supplemental workers. It also assumes that double the number of households proved able to succeed than actually did by way of creating their own jobs, and that all available jobs on offer got filled. If we further presume that all of the excluded primary earners should have made themselves equally competitive with the many supplemental earners occupying adequate jobs, even then the deficit in 1967 totaled more than 6 million jobs.

The architects of the War on Poverty were correct to conclude that the poor were handicapped and that they needed help. It erred in its most basic assumption that if workers were conscientious and persevering, the economy contained enough opportunity to absorb the large majority of them and to enable them to advance into the mainstream. Given the limited opportunities that were available, numerous workers found themselves employed in year-round full-time jobs at terribly low wages. More than 9 million year-round full-time workers occupied jobs at pay that fell short of an adequate wage. A large minority of them—nearly 3 million in 1967—were unable to lift their total household incomes up even to the government's woefully low poverty line, let alone to something close to a frugal mainstream lifestyle. Millions of other workers, unable to find full-time jobs, were employed only part-time. Without the availability of adequate jobs and industrious individuals' access to them, a War on Poverty could not render households economically independent and capable of moving into the mainstream.

Other workers—among them particularly those whose wage potential was closest to the bottom—decided to withdraw from the labor market in whole or in part, further undercutting the War on Poverty's ability to succeed. Blacks were undoubtedly in this position far more than whites. They received considerably lower wages than did whites even when at the same level of education and experience.[3] The incentives were meager. Starting in 1957 to 1960, prior to President Kennedy's inauguration, let alone the start of the War on Poverty in 1964–65 and the sharp expansion of welfare, the youngest among them who were just poised to enter the labor market began to decline participation in large numbers. The participation rate in the labor force among black males aged sixteen to twenty dropped by about 8 percent between 1956 and 1960, by 16 percent between 1956 and 1963, and by one quarter between 1956 and 1970 (participation among whites, who were less disadvantaged as a group, also receded, but more marginally).[4] Thereafter the participation of successive waves of young black male cohorts continued to decline. By the late 1950s and the early 1960s, civil rights sentiment and the consumer culture connected to television were becoming widespread. The disincentives and discouragement that poor economic rewards could be expected to produce, especially among those nearest to the bottom, conformed completely to the views of men such as Madison and Jefferson, who looked at poor economic conditions in the midst of surplus as having a potentially incendiary effect. Listen, though, to Adam Smith, who in *An Inquiry into the Nature and Causes of the Wealth of Nations* cautions: "The wages of labor are the encouragement of industry, which, like every other human quality, improves in proportion to the encouragement it receives. . . . Where wages are high, accordingly, we shall always find the workmen more active, diligent, and expeditious, than where they are low."[5] Labor must be rewarded decently, Smith warned, or else assiduousness among workers surely will suffer.[6] The severe shortage of decent jobs not only would stymie the War on Poverty's effectiveness in enabling households to become independent and to enter the mainstream; it would simultaneously undercut the program's capacity to prevent withdrawal from the labor force by less advantaged workers, a phenomenon for which the program itself soon was blamed. In a nation that presumed that enough opportunity existed, few ever noticed that the trend toward withdrawal from the labor force had antedated the antipoverty program by a number of years.

The undersupply of decent jobs posed serious issues in terms of the effectiveness of civil rights programs as well. Significant shortages of opportunity would render civil rights initiatives either impotent as a way to lift minorities to equal status within the mainstream; or, to the degree that equal opportunity was achieved and minorities secured mainstream jobs, that victory would narrow the number of adequate jobs available to whites, creating a hostile and debilitating backlash, and with it an ugly politics of anger and resentment. Either way, the outcome of civil rights programs would prove troubling. Bayard Rustin, a leading organizer of the March on Washington in 1963, observed that the constraints on opportunity were so substantial at that time as to handicap workers of all races even while affecting blacks disproportionately. Equal opportunity without sufficient opportunity, he said in 1965, was a recipe for failure if not complete disaster.[7] A 1968 analysis of jobs in New York City gave some particulars: it found that there were 5,000 job openings in total around the city for unskilled workers, including domestic service, at a time when the unemployed numbered almost 140,000 and more than 200,000 heads of household were on welfare.[8]

The circumstances that existed in the 1960s were never overcome, remaining much the same two decades later. An examination of job vacancies in New York City in 1989 showed, once again, the gravity of the situation. It concluded that there were 67,000 unfilled nonmanagement job vacancies available in all, over the whole year, for 770,000 economically disadvantaged adults eligible for job training, including recipients of welfare.[9] In Harlem in 1993, the ratio of applicants to hires was 14 to 1 even for entry-level jobs in fast food restaurants. The competition for jobs around the city was tough, the lines of workers seeking them long, and blacks similar to whites in education and experience were still at the end of the long queue.[10] And the pay for those jobs was nowhere near the wage needed for a worker to support an intact family with children at a minimally decent level, even assuming the other partner was also employed.

Either very considerable wage raises or the increased availability of far better jobs would be required in order for workers like these to feel that they could support a family decently, including taking into account the help of earnings from a partner. A national study of the wage mobility of newly hired low-wage workers regardless of race, published by the Congressional Budget Office during the early 1990s, found that after a year of employment workers who kept on the job had gotten wage improvements that on average surpassed inflation only if the workers had completed college. Even those workers with some college education only managed, on average, to keep up with inflation.[11] This simply reflected the larger picture extending over the prior two decades. Many workers experienced no wage mobility, even if they had some college education or had earned a technical degree beyond high school, over the entire period. As we observed in Chapter 5, a majority of low-paid heads of household were unable to raise themselves to an adequate wage even if they worked year-round full-time every year, including those with some college education.[12]

The War on Poverty and action on civil rights comprised the nation's main lines of attack against the problems of economic disadvantage and blocked mobility. Both initiatives made inclusion within the mainstream their avowed objective,[13] and both initiatives presumed that sufficient opportunity existed in the economy for conscientious and persevering households not simply to get jobs but, over time, to lift themselves into the mainstream. Yet with a scarcity of adequate jobs, millions of households continued to remain outside the margins, *whether they worked or not.* In the face of this disturbing situation, the government started to increase social spending not simply for nonworking households but at an even faster pace for working families. Commencing in the late 1960s, programs such as food stamps and, later, the earned income tax credit began to grant billions of dollars of social assistance to working families. By 1990 the amount of assistance made available to working families through these two programs alone surpassed the amount spent by the federal government on welfare's centerpiece, Aid to Families with Dependent Children (AFDC). The scarcity of decent jobs had another side effect: as we have seen, the experience of blocked mobility affected work effort itself, with the result that the participation of disadvantaged workers in the labor force started to decline. Faced with these developments, the public soon came to see the programs as boondoggles and failures, and the focus of national debate increasingly turned away from the question of how to positively attack economic disadvantage and toward an attack on the War on Poverty and the very idea of the welfare state. Many accused the so-called safety net known as welfare of itself causing labor force withdrawal and idleness and so sentencing its recipients to generations of entrenched economic immobility.

Concerns about the counterproductive effects of anti-poverty "handouts" and the whole welfare system developed over time into an overriding political issue powering the election campaigns of candidates and even the identities of political parties. Richard Nixon's searing attacks on the War on Poverty helped bring him to victory in 1968 and 1972. Ronald Reagan's disparaging remarks about lazy welfare cheats and the nonworking poor took center stage in his victorious campaigns of 1980 and 1984. In the view of Democratic Senator Daniel Patrick Moynihan, promises of fundamental welfare reform provided the vital key to victory for the Clinton election campaign in 1992.[14] Clinton aides themselves estimated that fully 40 percent of his paid advertisements mentioned ending welfare in its current form.[15] Three years later, in 1995, following the Republican congressional landslide and the ouster of the Democrats from power, newly elected Senator Rick Santorum of Pennsylvania underscored the depth of feeling the issue aroused on the Republican side. It had become nothing less than a matter of political identity. Many Republican senators, he said, considered welfare reform to be "the defining issue of who we are as a party."[16] By the 1990s Americans had grown weary and deeply resentful, and were nearly unanimous in their belief that the welfare system had to be overhauled. To many Americans, the growth of welfare and welfare dependency signaled a disturbing decay in the moral character of the populace. That welfare assistance perpetuated poverty had become the common view. The whole system promoted idleness and irresponsibility, and at budget-busting public expense. It was not enough that adults on welfare ought to be required to learn a job or skill;[17] in addition, a large majority of the public believed that after a limited time period on the welfare rolls all able-bodied recipients (including women with preschool children) should be required to find gainful employment.[18]

How did welfare become such a mess, the cause of so much ill will and resentment? The public's view about the purpose of the welfare system was straightforward enough. To the average American, welfare ought to meet stop-gap needs in order to assist families during temporary hard times to get back on their feet and become self-supporting. Welfare ought to be transitional. It was meant to be a second chance, not a way of life.[19]

But for this philosophy to succeed, for welfare to be transitional, an alternative had to exist. Opportunities for hardworking households to afford a minimally adequate level of living had to be available. Yet given the dearth of jobs capable of supporting families, many recipients of welfare have come to believe that they cannot live minimally decently by way of employment alone, and the wages employment pays. As economist Robert Haveman concludes: "The evidence is strong that women currently on welfare and likely to be applying for assistance in the future will not be able to earn nearly enough to support their families. Indeed, if they are required to pay for the child care necessitated by full-time work, they will have to commit nearly half of their take-home pay simply to cover the care of their children while they are at work."[20] At the same time, recipients of welfare also know that welfare assistance, by itself, is inadequate unless they get the full package of benefits (fewer than one third of them do), if even then. So, often they combine welfare with work. As Sharita Hargrove, a welfare mother living in Kansas City, told *The New York Times*, "I've been employed forever even if it was under the table."[21] Even before welfare's reform in 1996, some estimates indicate that nearly half of all recipients combined the income available from welfare with additional income from jobs, often doing various kinds of part-time work under the table in order to make ends meet.[22]

The logical next step for these recipients, it might seem, would be to find and accept full-time jobs in order to get off of the welfare rolls. Historically, about one third of all recipients have been on welfare only temporarily. They then leave the rolls permanently by way of taking a job or getting married. This is not to say that they have joined the mainstream, or are about to, however. Consider the example of Linda Baldwin, of Chicago, who left welfare to take up a year-round full-time job as a counselor in a youth center.[23] By her third year of steady employment, sometimes working ten to twelve hours a day, she nevertheless earned $3,000 a year *beneath* the official federal poverty line, fully $9,000 below a base-line income. Despite working full-time and more, she had to rely on nearly $3,000 in food stamps over the year and approximately another $2,000 a year in housing subsidies. Even with $5,000 of assistance added to her earnings, she and her children continued to have to live in a drug- and gang-infested slum neighborhood. She could not afford the rent elsewhere. She could not afford the eyeglasses her son badly needed for school. Unable to pay $50 to visit a dentist, she went to work every day enduring the pain in a severely aching tooth.

Ms. Baldwin is among a minority of recipients under the unreformed system who left the welfare rolls by way of employment or marriage.[24] The remainder, to whom the reforms of welfare in 1996 were directed, divided into recipients who were on and off welfare intermittently and recipients who had become dependent upon welfare.

The experiences of women like Linda Baldwin, along with the lack of any meaningful upward mobility for many millions of capable and experienced full-time workers over prolonged periods of time, form the context facing many of the mothers who remained on the welfare rolls continuously, year after year. The majority of all long-term welfare recipients, then and undoubtedly still today, rank in the bottom fifth of the nation on aptitude tests,[25] significantly below the aptitude of manual workers—the occupation that scores at the bottom of the labor force in mean aptitude.[26] It is tough for them to get through high school, and many of them have no high school degree. Their capacity to compete is very low. Partly as a result of economic disadvantage, coupled with other reasons, a number of them are emotionally disturbed as well. They are the least competitive facing a serious undersupply of adequate jobs, in a world that often leaves even adept and experienced workers in malevolent hardship even after very long periods of time; is it any wonder that they might rely on assistance to the point where, as one welfare case manager described it, "it scares them to death to try to get off it?"[27] What alternative, realistically, does the economy leave them with? One might argue, from a principle of reciprocity, that if persons of low aptitude cannot contribute much in a competitive economy, they are not deserving of societal returns in any case. Yet as we observed in Chapter 3, if the equal moral worth of individuals is a guideline, or the inculcation of values such as the work ethic is a goal, then providing individuals with the opportunity to attain independence through work or other means must enjoy priority over the objective of sheer reciprocity, let alone acceptance of market outcomes, which are often in error, as a determinative measure of desert.

Prior to the 1996 reforms, experiments in states all across the nation had underscored the difficulty of moving households off welfare and into independence when low-paying and unsteady jobs are all that is available, and sometimes not even these. Without statutory cutoffs, the most successful experiments had a hard time reducing the welfare caseload by as much as 20 percent. Even among households that left the welfare rolls, the programs ended up getting no more than a small handful of them up to the official federal poverty line, let alone anywhere near a base-line standard of living. Robert Rector of the Heritage Foundation was brutally frank in describing the results of the most effective reform programs: "At best, they get a 16 percent reduction in caseload," he said. "This is scarcely ending welfare as we know it."[28] Of course statutory cutoffs may accomplish the goal of forcing recipient families off welfare, but they do nothing to address the shortages of adequate opportunity facing these families or the problem of economic disadvantage, or to control the variety of dysfunctional behaviors to which serious economic disadvantage contributes.

Needless to say, the public wants far greater progress than a 15 percent caseload reduction, and surely does not want to subsidize idleness. But the public is also quite discerning. While a substantial majority of the public supports a two-year cutoff of welfare, backing among Americans for such a policy plummets to only one quarter of the public if the available jobs pay "low wages that would make it difficult to support a family." Still fewer people, less than one fifth of the public, favor a welfare cutoff if the recipient cannot locate a job.[29] That decent employment alternatives be available is vital to any effective answer in the public's mind.

The shortages of adequate jobs have done more than sorely complicate the problem of solving welfare dependency; they have also had a strong influence on those behaviors that have led families onto the welfare rolls in the first place. One of the most crucial is teenage childbearing. Among all mothers under age thirty who are on welfare, fully 60 percent first gave birth as teenagers. These same recipients are also the most likely to become dependent upon welfare for long periods of time.[30] Of all children living in poverty in the United States, nearly half were born to a teenage parent.

Serious shortages of economic opportunities have an effect on the perceptions and mental constructs of teenagers, who naturally think (even if only hazily) in terms of the opportunities that are available to them. If few or none exist, many will conclude that one cannot get ahead by one's own efforts, at least not using conventional methods. Back in the mid-1960s, the view of a sizable number of young persons that opportunity was in short supply[31] was broadly accurate. Just as Daniel Patrick Moynihan was about to publish his book alerting the public to the fracture of the black family, in 1965, Kenneth Clark described the alarming incidence of illegitimate teenage births then occurring among blacks:

In the ghetto, the meaning of the illegitimate child is not ultimate disgrace. There is not the demand for abortion or for surrendering the child that one finds in more privileged communities. In the middle class, the disgrace of illegitimacy is tied to personal and family aspirations. In lower-class families, on the other hand, the girl loses only some of her already limited opportunities by having an illegitimate child; she is not going to get a "better marriage" or improve her economic social status either way. On the contrary, a child is a symbol of the fact that she is a woman, and she may gain from having something of her own. Nor is the boy who fathers an illegitimate child going to lose, for where is he going?[32]

The consequences of the dearth of opportunity for the behavior of teenagers who *retained* mainstream aspirations might not be any better. In 1965 Bayard Rustin wrote from personal observation:

From the point of view of motivation, some of the healthiest Negro youngsters I know are juvenile delinquents: vigorously pursuing the American Dream of material acquisition and status, yet finding the conventional means of attaining it blocked off, they do not yield to defeatism but resort to illegal (and often ingenious) methods.[33]

This mind-set among delinquents, he warned, was a consequence not merely of the unequal treatment accorded to blacks but of an absolute lack of appropriate opportunity confronting workers of all races, albeit disproportionately among blacks.[34]

Of course, economic hardship was nothing new in the United States. Yet, once again, it had rather different ramifications for a country entering a new age, during the 1950s and 1960s, where the mythic frontier, with its promise of untold opportunity and new life for the poor, had vanished entirely from memory at the same time that the fires of mainstream aspirations were stoked to an unparalleled degree by the ideology of the civil rights movement and the introduction of television. The shortages of opportunity able to provide a minimally decent living which American families encountered daily, on a scale numbering in the millions of jobs, stood in sharp contrast with these circumstances.

The occurrence of teenage illegitimacy, already creeping upward in the 1950s, started to soar during the early 1960s.[35] In 1965 there were 130,000 illegitimate births, a 41 percent increase over 1960. By 1990 the number of unwed teenage births surged past 350,000 a year, almost three times the incidence in 1965. Teenage childbearing was concentrated most heavily within populations of youths from poor families:[36] of all teenage illegitimate births, about half were to adolescents from families in the lowest quarter of the income scale.[37] Elijah Anderson, professor of sociology at the University of Pennsylvania, who began studying low-income neighborhoods in depth more than two decades ago, has found the constriction of opportunity and the incidence of unwed teenage childbearing to be closely connected. "Middle-class youths take a strong interest in their future and know what pregnancy can do to derail that future," he pointed out. "In contrast, the [inner-city] adolescent sees no future to derail, no hope for a tomorrow very different from today, hence, little to lose by having an out-of-wedlock child."[38] Taking up this view, Douglas Besharov, a resident scholar at the American Enterprise Institute, observed in late 1993: "The association between poverty, poor school performance and poor life prospects on the one side and out-of-wedlock births on the other is too obvious to ignore."[39]

Dearth of opportunity is linked to teenage illegitimacy in a number of ways. Only one of them (and not necessarily the most important) is the familiar problem of the limited supply of marriageable male partners who can support a family. Another is the commonsense proposition, supported by sociological studies, that scarcity of opportunity erodes young people's confidence that they can make it into the mainstream, and therefore their motivation to achieve.[40] Regardless of aptitude, students who think it unlikely that they will ever get a good job do less well in school and drop out sooner.[41] Women are concerned not merely with the economic prospects of males but with the meaningfulness of their own prospects for success in the economy;[42] if their prospects are slim, motherhood, even as a single parent, becomes a more attractive option for self-fulfillment.[43] And among adolescent black males in the inner city, Anderson found that the lack of decent opportunity to attain jobs able to support a family—the conventional symbol of adult manhood—leads to an increasing emphasis on sexual prowess and assertiveness as a measure of manhood, with babies as the proof.[44] Amid a dearth of opportunity, the various forces interact and combine to produce a substantial effect on unwed teen childbearing.

While teenage childbearing can be a cause of poverty and lack of opportunity, the reverse occurs much more frequently than is commonly understood: poverty and lack of opportunity are a cause of teenage childbearing. Arline Geronimus and Sanders Korenman compared long-term economic and health outcomes—using sisters in order to control for the effects of many other variables often said to be important—of women who gave birth as teenagers and those who postponed first births to their twenties or beyond. There was little difference in outcome between the two groups of sisters; those who delayed childbirth into their twenties did not thereby, in general, become any better off.[45] Kristin Luker's analysis reached the same conclusion: most teenage childbearers would have fared about as poorly even had they postponed childbearing.[46] Frank Furstenberg, Jr., of the University of Pennsylvania put it this way: "Early childbearing owes its persistence to the fact that many women—not just disadvantaged black youth—have relatively little to lose by having a first birth in their teens or early 20s. . . . The incentives for postponing parenthood are only substantial if young women really believe that they have a strong prospect for making it into the middle class."[47] Given a shortage of decent jobs coupled with the absence of income mobility into the mainstream for a substantial number of experienced and capable workers who do hold jobs, many adolescents who live in poverty—particularly those at lower levels of aptitude—correctly perceive that the chances for them are slim at best. They are being realistic. Under the prevailing conditions they look for other avenues to meaningful lives.

Other forces have also given rise to the growth of teenage illegitimacy: powerful changes in the culture and morality have reduced the social stigma attendant on out-of-wedlock births and have nearly eliminated the stigma attached to premarital sex. These attitudes have reached beyond the poor and now extend to all income levels.[48] Dramatic shifts in thinking such as these are a part of the context in which the rise of unwed teenage childbearing has taken place, but they do not explain why—despite the now widespread acceptance of premarital sex within all income levels—childbearing among teenagers remains significantly correlated with youth poverty. Nor do differences in access to information about sex or birth control provide an effective explanation for this correlation.[49] The fact is that those adolescents who have the least to lose, or perceive they do, are the most likely to bear children.

Some observers claim that welfare has provided women with economic choices that would not have been open to them otherwise, and that the substantial increase in welfare assistance, beginning in the mid-1960s, led to the rise in the rate of teenage illegitimate childbearing.[50] As welfare benefits became a more viable alternative economically, the argument goes, reliance upon assistance started to grow. In its wake, the culture of work and of legitimacy in childbearing began to erode, and nonwork and illegitimate childbearing increasingly became socially accepted behaviors, leading to an escalation in illegitimacy, in the number of households taking up welfare, and in the length of time households remained dependent upon welfare.[51] Of course, the fact is that teenage illegitimacy's surge from 1960 through 1964 preceded the huge expansion in assistance to individual welfare families that took place after 1965 through the Great Society, not the other way around.[52]

The connection between welfare benefit levels and out-of-wedlock births has been the subject of numerous studies. The large majority of these studies conclude that the size of welfare benefits has little to do with the incidence of premarital childbearing.[53] Among the lower forty-eight states, none grants welfare benefit packages bringing recipient families near to a base-line income.[54] Apart from that, assistance levels vary significantly among the individual states, in some cases by more than 70 percent.[55] Nonetheless, states with the lowest benefit levels generally experience rates of out-of-wedlock births broadly similar to those of states with the highest benefit levels. The sizable differences in state benefits account for no more than 12 percent of illegitimacy among whites and even less among blacks.[56] Similarly, assistance levels have had little effect on overall welfare caseloads. Five states today have assistance levels low enough (combining AFDC, food stamps, and Medicaid) that the benefits fall below two thirds of the official poverty line.[57] Yet in 1992 more than 1.6 million people a month were recipients of welfare in these five states. The incidence of welfare recipiency in these states with the lowest benefits amounted to about 5 percent of their total populations, exactly the same proportion as for the nation as a whole.

The fact that large variations in welfare levels have had little influence on illegitimacy suggests that in the absence of a positive economic option, an outright cutoff of benefits might reduce illegitimacy to some degree but will not cut deeply into it. Most of these parents and their children will live in more dire circumstances still, as they have done in response to the real decline in welfare benefits that has already taken place over the past twenty years and as they did from 1960 to 1965 during the initial surge in illegitimacy, prior to the jump in welfare benefits after 1965. In 1960 the welfare package, even in a relatively generous state like Pennsylvania, came to less than half the poverty line.[58] The remedy of an outright cutoff also fails to address the crucial practical and moral issue of how the children in these families will fare following the cutoff of benefits if the parent has been unable to locate steady or decent-paid work. And it fails to address the larger philosophical issue of whether it is right to permit a condition to continue in which the opportunity simply does not exist for many to make a minimally respectable living, consigning those left out with no alternative except to live in degrading circumstances. Providing a positive option—the opportunity to make a decent living—is an essential missing element in most policy discussions. Surely it is among the vital ingredients of a solution. As Douglas Besharov noted: "[Supplying] a good education and real opportunities in life are the best contraceptives."[59]

Juvenile delinquency and crime, too, began to skyrocket during the 1960s, creating an increasingly violent and dangerous society. Soaring to new record heights during the decade of the 1970s, rates have since remained close to those high levels despite the substantial declines that favorable demographic factors—particularly the passage of the baby boom generation beyond their prime crime-producing years of fourteen to twenty-four and into middle age—should have led us to expect.

The connection between rates of juvenile delinquency and crime, on the one hand, and the level of economic opportunity and poverty on the other, is far from a one-to-one relationship, but numerous linkages do exist. As in the case of teenage childbearing, the most obvious link concerns the way an environment of constricted opportunity shapes the alternatives that are available—or are perceived to be available—in people's lives. In the latter half of the 1960s, nearly three fifths of adolescents and young adults in hardened inner cities who were surveyed believed that the opportunity to attain decent jobs simply did not exist.[60] Considering the acute shortage of adequate jobs that these youths faced, for a large number of them, even if they worked steadily and hard, that perception held true. In addition, workers occupying low-wage employment and unstable jobs tend to develop comparatively shallow social ties either with co-workers or to their places of employment, leaving them with a still-smaller stake in conformity. If an outlook stripped of hope and devoid of firm ties to co-workers and workplace combines with debilitating family circumstances in which parental or other familial disapproval is considered no more than a small cost, individuals then have precious few restraints. Those who feel like outsiders and to act like outsiders and to engage in a wide variety of delinquent behaviors, whether for money or not.

According to surveys of disadvantaged black young males in 1989, a clear majority—about three fifths—said they could earn more from crime than they could in the legal labor market.[61] Nearly 40 percent reported that they had opportunities to make illegal income several times a day. One inner-city adolescent, a white male, gives his view: "Out here, there's not the opportunity to make money. That's how you get into stealin' and all that shit."[62] Among black sixteen-to-twenty-four-year-olds surveyed who engaged in crime, average earnings came to $19 per hour—nearly four times what they would have been able to take home from legitimate work.[63] One can surmise that the effect of these circumstances on adolescents who already feel like outsiders and have few controlling influences would be substantial. In-depth interviews with such inner-city teenagers led criminologist Jeffrey Fagan of Rutgers University to observe that for them, "the choice between lousy jobs and short-term gains and crime is pretty clear. Kids told us over and over again that they had no vision of the future."[64] For inner-city teenagers who perceive bleak prospects and have few counterbalancing ties, economists George Peterson and Wayne Vroman suggest that the economic reality of low-wage dead-end jobs results in the adolescents making what they see as a rational choice to engage in illegal activity.[65] The conclusion that a connection exists between constricted opportunity and the incidence of delinquency is supported by evidence from a variety of different approaches and an array of databases.[66] It is a conclusion reminiscent of Rustin's observations in 1965 about the inner-city mentality, which, he concluded, prompted rational and enterprising adolescents to engage in crime.[67]

In this context, too, the power of television cannot be ignored. No one is more aware of the dynamic than the secondary school teacher. According to R Baird Shuman of the University of Illinois: "Adolescents who see no reasonable hope of attaining by socially acceptable means the levels of life regularly portrayed on television and [in] many movies are vulnerable to pressures that entice them into such illegal yet lucrative activities as theft, drug pushing, or prostitution. These are the realities with which secondary school teachers and administrators constantly deal."[68] A north Philadelphia hustler points out how television makes expensive goods fashionable in low-income neighborhoods: "It's like the sneaker commercials on TV that say they can make you run faster and jump higher. The kids all want them. But basically, they all come from single-parent homes. Some of the parents are on welfare, others work. You got . . . hungry kids that are willing to sell drugs all night and all day to get some Adidases or some other brand-name stuff. This is the only way they're going to get it."[69]

The dearth of opportunity that defines the environment is a function not so much of the sheer unavailability of jobs as of the lack of jobs that pay decently. Among adolescents and young adults, levels of crime appear to be related less significantly to the rate of unemployment than to the rate at which workers *are* employed but in low-wage jobs.[70] Many readers will be surprised to learn that 70 percent of all offenders incarcerated in state prisons were gainfully employed, and not unemployed or out of the labor market altogether, at the time of their arrest.[71] The lack of meaningful opportunity and not simply unemployment establishes the economic context. During the 1980s and early 1990s, crime rates remained close to record levels (three times what they had been in the early 1960s) even though a significant drop should have been expected due to the declining proportion of the population in the fourteen-to-twenty-four age group representing the prime crime-producing years *and* a substantially reduced rate of unemployment in those years.[72] That opportunities for adequate jobs and mobility remained in extremely short supply throughout the period may help to explain why.

The mentality that sees crime as a rational choice in the face of a scarcity of meaningful legal alternatives presumably would apply most strongly to persons having the least prospects on average—that is, to persons who are at the lowest levels of aptitude. The linkage between low IQ and teenage crime is indeed a close and frequently documented one. Numerous sociologists have concluded that blocked opportunity is an important part of the explanation. In the words of Christopher Jencks of Northwestern University, "Adolescents with low IQs commit crimes not because they are inherently more hostile, amoral, or impulsive than their high-IQ classmates, but because both schools and labor markets treat them in ways that make them hostile, amoral, and impulsive. . . . In [market competitive] societies like our own, youngsters with low IQs cannot do much that others value."[73]

Economic prospects and circumstances affect juvenile delinquency more than by helping shape the choice structure that people face in their lives; they also do so by influencing the family structure that molds and socializes the values of children and how they make their choices. The strains associated with economic hardship can give rise to debilitating family dynamics. Having an upbringing in a disrupted family is known to be one of the strongest correlates of crime. About 70 percent of all juvenile offenders in state institutions come from fatherless homes.[74] Scarce economic opportunity creates a context in which fatherless families stemming from illegitimate childbearing are especially likely to occur.[75] Fatherless families resulting from divorce also bear some connection to economic deprivation: partly due to the economic stresses, intact families living in poverty dissolve at double the rate of families above the poverty level. In addition, research shows that a good part of the heightened deviant behaviors associated with adolescents from divorced families can be accounted for by the altered economic circumstances following divorce, particularly the limited earnings capacity of many single parents and the resultant disproportionate loss of income created by the divorce.[76] The lowered level of parental supervision often found in these families accounts for much of the rest.

The entire period of the past three decades suffered a serious deficit of jobs. As the jaws of economic scarcity tightened during those years, half of all experienced workers found their economic progress completely stymied even if they were steadily employed. A lack of jobs paying minimally adequate wages, choking opportunity, left millions of households marginalized. At the same time, Americans witnessed a seemingly relentless rise of serious social problems and the apparent incapacity of government to address these problems effectively, whether it be poverty, welfare reciprocity and dependency, teenage illegitimacy, family disruption, or juvenile delinquency and crime. By the early 1990s a child growing up in America was several times more likely to be killed by gunfire than was a child living in the war zone that was Northern Ireland.

Chapter 8

GOVERNMENT, THE ECONOMY, AND ECONOMIC OPPORTUNITY

I t should come as no surprise that the combination of constricted economic opportunity and rising social disorder deeply affected the confidence Americans placed in politics and in their political institutions. In the 1950s loyalties to political parties embraced about three out of every four members of the public. A large majority of Americans believed themselves to be "Democrats" or "Republicans," often strongly so. Over the next three decades, these loyalties weakened to the point where Americans' strongest political allegiances are now to "none of the above." By the late 1980s, for the first time, "independent" had become the nation's largest political party.[1] The confidence and trust of the public in government plummeted to low depths during the days of Vietnam and Watergate, but the twenty years thereafter have hardly proved restorative. Now, however, the absence of confidence and trust in political institutions expressed by more than two thirds of Americans is no longer in reaction to a specific issue or scandal but to a generalized, seemingly permanent state of affairs. With the erosion of confidence, fewer voters have shown up at the polls. Growing more cynical, Americans have increasingly come to believe that government itself causes and perpetuates their problems. Numerous governmental programs have become seen as expensive failures. More is at stake than a mere loss of confidence. Few more incendiary contexts exist that are able, if sparked, to fuel the onset of extremism, unrest, and ultimately political instability than the evaporation of conventional political moorings coupled with the growth of popular alienation and anger. Far from being "of the people," government is ever more becoming seen as the people's enemy.

The founders believed that the federal government had a crucial role to play in fostering the level of economic opportunity necessary to enable Americans to attain independence and a decent livelihood. The same principle animated the Republican party that nominated Abraham Lincoln.[2] The 1860 party platform called for the federal government's passage of the Homestead Act, granting free land in the West to many thousands of families which enabled them to provide decent livelihoods for themselves, and it urged federal support for the building of railroads and other improvements that would bolster the nation's economic development.[3]

Since 1960 spending by the federal government as a proportion of the total economy, measured by the GNP, rose from 18.9 percent to 22.8 percent. During the same period, many Americans came to believe that, far from facilitating the rise of new opportunity, government now stood in the way of prosperity—that its escalating spending, taxation, regulation, and waste were strangling the growth of business and the economy. This thesis has become a politically powerful way of explaining the economic stagnation and loss of opportunity that many households have experienced over the past two decades. The route to a return of prosperity and opportunity, this line of argument contends, is to rein in the nation's government.

Yet this popular argument ignores the crucial fact that the economy *did* generate an enormous amount of new opportunity after 1970: nearly 16 million net new year-round full-time jobs paying at least a base-line wage or better between 1970 and 1990—a 35 percent expansion in the number of such jobs in those twenty years alone. This was a phenomenal performance, far surpassing anything the Europeans were able to accomplish, in any individual country or in all the countries combined. As discussed in Chapter 5, the growing shortfall in adequate jobs resulted from an extraordinarily rapid increase in the demand for these jobs from about 23 million new households and supplemental earners during the same years.

Would the economy have performed even more powerfully and created still greater prosperity and opportunity had the growth of government been more effectively restrained? "The era of big government is over," President Clinton said in his 1996 State of the Union address, echoing what had become an increasingly insistent Republican theme ever since the Goldwater wing took over the Republican party in 1964. Believers found a resonant slogan in Ronald Reagan's first inaugural address: "Government is not the solution to our problem. Government is the problem,"[4] he said. Announcing his own bid for the presidency in 1995, Robert Dole reiterated the message: "Let us rein in our government to set the spirit of the American people free."[5] Soon thereafter Dole described the struggle against the power of the federal government as "the last great crusade of this century."[6] Fighting for the Republican nomination in 1996, Steve Forbes called the government's role in the economy "political repression."[7] In 1996 the Republican party itself asserted: "Big government, high taxes and excessive red tape are what stands between working Americans and better jobs and a higher standard of living."[8]

The claim that the government and its bureaucracy have grown excessively burdensome on the economy and become a heavy constraint on opportunity is an apparently compelling one. It seems to be supported by both logic and evidence. Government spends the taxpayers' money. If one is spending other people's money, it is merely rational, Milton and Rose Friedman point out, to want to spend as much as one can without paying close attention to the level of waste in one's spending.[9] Using other people's money gives government an incentive to spend more than it needs to, and this incentive to spend is reinforced by the natural bureaucratic drive for power. The result is that government tends to swell in size, budgetary spending grows out of proportion to the economy, and the government crowds out the private sector, especially since there exists no effective check on government comparable to the disciplinary imperatives of competition in the business world.

The logic behind the theory is plausible. It just doesn't happen to correspond to reality. The argument that government has a natural impulse toward growth presumably applies to most governmental activities, not solely to a selected few, yet actual spending growth by the federal government over the years has been confined to a narrow and highly defined set of activities, mainly Social Security and Medicare. These insurance programs are financed separately by a Social Security tax; they have grown in order to provide a basic level of income and medical support for the retired elderly and to reduce the financial dependency of the elderly on their children. Notwithstanding the programs' growth, nearly all sides of the debate agree that these programs ought to be protected from real (inflation-adjusted) cuts. General revenue programs like defense, national security, foreign aid, welfare and public assistance, Medicaid, education, worker training, police and the justice system, farm subsidies, energy, highways and mass transportation, space exploration, parks, regulatory actions, research, grants-in-aid to the states, interest on the debt, and so forth—all of which rely upon the general revenue taxes (personal income taxes, corporate taxes, excise taxes, and tariff receipts)—are the areas people usually have in mind when they think about the bureaucracies and the "dead weight" of government. And contrary to a virtually universal popular view, what the federal government spends in all these areas combined (that is, all areas except for Social Security and Medicare) has remained very much the same relative to the size of the GNP as it was during the Eisenhower years, *prior* to the Kennedy presidency: 15.8 percent of the GNP in 1955 and 15.6 percent in 1960; 16.1 percent of the GNP in 1980; and, 16.4 percent of the GNP in 1990.[10] Something—very possibly checks and balances—operated to restrain spending reasonably well in these areas.

The same is the case with taxation: taxes did not grow, save for those related to the social insurance programs. In fact, all federal taxes, excluding those for the insurance programs, amounted to 14.6 percent of the GNP in 1960; by 1990 they had dropped to 10.9 percent of the GNP.[11] Outside the insurance programs, federal taxation (the bulk of it coming from personal income and corporate profits taxes along with excise taxes) diminished by 3.7 percent relative to the size of the economy.

Had the level of general revenue taxation remained the same proportion of the economy as in 1960, federal government revenue in 1990 would have closed the deficit by $214 billion, leaving only $7 billion of the total $221.5 billion deficit recorded for that year.[12]

Expansion of government comes in many guises, of course. The regulatory tentacles of government may involve little direct governmental expenditure or taxation but reach out to impose a variety of restrictions and spending obligations on business and other economic activities. Widely cited figures put the total cost of regulation for the nation in the early 1990s at nearly $330 billion,[13] only a tiny fraction of it spent directly by the government. According to the same study, the cost of regulation in 1979 was about $160 billion[14]—seeming to signify a doubling in the regulatory burden over a handful of years. Yet if we take into account the growth of the economy over those years, the cost of government regulation rose only proportionately. In fact, at $330 billion during 1990, the cost of regulation actually consumed slightly less of the GNP (by about a half percent) that year than was the case in 1979.[15]

What about earlier years? Much regulation concerning environmental pollution, consumer protection, and safety in the workplace began coming into force in the early 1970s and had huge rates of growth during the half decade leading up to 1980, moderating thereafter. But the federal government also curtailed a number of other regulatory efforts in those years, especially industry-specific regulation and financial regulation; as a result, the overall costs of regulation remained a similar proportion of GNP.[16]

So, compared to other nations, how burdensome is governmental spending, taxation, and regulation, taken together, on economic activity in the United States? In 1995 the Heritage

Foundation, a leading conservative think tank, looked into this question by examining ten broad areas of governmental involvement in the economy, covering the first half of the 1990s, in order to compile what it called the "Index of Economic Freedom." The United States ranked as the highest (most "free") of any major Western industrialized country on the index—ahead of West Germany, ahead even of Japan. Only three of the 101 jurisdictions measured ranked ahead of the United States,[17] all of them quasi-city-states: Hong Kong, Singapore, and Bahrain. Not a single one of the twelve other Western industrialized nations analyzed enjoyed a lower level of taxation; only one nation (Great Britain) experienced a lower level of regulation; and only one (Japan) had a lower level of governmental expenditure.[18]

As for the presumption that government has a tendency to balloon toward higher levels of *inefficient* spending and waste compared to the private sector, measures of worker efficiency or productivity (output per hour of labor) applied to federal agencies since 1967 disclose that productivity levels in government and in the business sector have risen at about the same rate.[19] Overall productivity improvement in the private sector has not exceeded that of the government.

Some will retort that the government is productive of "make-work," of unnecessary activity that we could easily do without. Nearly everyone has his or her own favorite examples. Generally, however, this argument revolves around differences of opinion over what is and is not useful; around issues of values, not mainly around questions of efficiency.

This is not to say that no waste exists in government and its bureaucracies (it would be equally foolish to say that no waste exists in private business and its bureaucracies). But it is important to understand that assertions about extraordinary government waste are mostly built upon anecdotes, *not on a body of rig-orous evidence*. Hard evidence analyzing the relative efficiency of the public and private sectors is difficult to find; it requires not only comparing government agencies and private businesses operating in precisely the same areas of service or production, but also comparing a large number of cases in order to hold constant the wide array of potentially distorting variables. The best conclusion that can be reached based on the available evidence is that more variation probably exists *within* both the public-sector sphere and the private-sector sphere than occurs between them. While a majority of private-sector enterprises appear to operate with somewhat less waste, the differences are often small and there are significant exceptions—with sanitation and waste disposal services, for example, some public enterprises operate far more efficiently than do most private concerns.[20]

Exaggerated claims about government inefficiency and waste are apt to take hold quickly, however, in a society already prone to believe that government has a natural tendency toward runaway spending growth. In the late 1970s Milton and Rose Friedman concluded that the federal government was spending so much money on programs to assist the poor that its total expenditures came to *twice* the amount needed to raise every poor American above the poverty line.[21] This kind of excess, they said, is exactly what results from government's natural tendency to grow and spend wastefully. In 1978, the Friedmans pointed out, the government poured $90 billion into need-based public assistance programs. The Census Bureau estimated that there then were about 25 million poor Americans. The amount spent by the need-based programs thus came to about $3,500 per poor American, or around $14,000 for a family of four. The federal poverty line in 1978, they observed, was only about $7,000 for a family of four, merely half as much. The claim that the government was spending twice the amount needed to lift every American above the poverty line seemed an unavoidable conclusion.

Where did the excess of assistance go? According to the Friedmans, a fair amount of it went to pay "administrative expenditures, supporting a massive bureaucracy at attractive pay scales."[22] In addition, some of it was spent on recipients who could not be regarded as poor by any reasonable definition. Still another segment went to welfare cheats. The combination of these misdirected funds, the Friedmans argued, caused taxpayers to have to pay twice the amount demonstrably needed to deal effectively with the problem of poverty. Such conclusions, coupled with Reaganesque images of welfare queens, were readily embraced by a popular audience already angered by the seeming relentless growth of governmental spending and taxation.

Examining a number of complications in these claims leads to a far more reasonable explanation, however. Let's start with the actual figures: the poverty line for 1978 for a family of four was $6,662; the total amount of government spending on all need-based assistance for that year was $82.6 billion.[23]

Yet quite a few of the assistance programs were never intended to deliver families out of poverty by raising actual income, as presumed by the Friedmans. Take, for example, health programs such as Medicaid, which provide essential services that the poor could not otherwise afford, but have no effect on income enabling a family to rise above the federally defined poverty line. Likewise, programs such as Head Start and the Pell Grants are expected to help individuals get ahead economically some years down the road, or to prevent them from ever becoming poor in the first place, rather than to improve individuals' current incomes in the short-term manner suggested by the Friedmans. Such need-based health, education, and training programs, combined, amounted to about $34 billion in 1978, leaving a total expenditure of $48.6 billion on actual income assistance directed to low-income persons. About $9.3 billion of this money went to low-income persons who were above the federal poverty line, since eligibility for food stamps, housing assistance, and sometimes even welfare itself does not end abruptly at the poverty line but is phased out as other household income rises. A complete cutoff of assistance whenever a family reaches the poverty line would mean that a family would not be able to lift its income above the poverty line even if it worked longer hours or earned a raise in pay, thereby eliminating incentives to work harder.[24] The remaining $39.3 billion was spent on the 25.4 million Americans in households the Census Bureau identified as poor: a cost of about $1,550 per poor American, or $6,200 for a family of four—below the poverty line of $6,662 *even before* one subtracts for reasonable bureaucratic costs, which at 10 percent would bring the family total to about $5,600.[25]

Remember the story President Reagan told of the high-riding welfare queen from Chicago who cheated the government out of $150,000 by using scores of different names and addresses, a dozen Social Security cards, and several fake deceased husbands? "The only factual basis for that story," journalist Daniel Schorr reported, "was a woman who was convicted of fraud for using two false names to collect a total of $8,000."[26]

The public is very quick to believe that government spends a lot more than it actually does, especially in areas citizens may consider secondary. Three quarters of the public believes that the government spends too much money on foreign aid; their estimate is that it represents about 15 percent of the federal budget. In reality, less than 1 percent goes to foreign aid, while the public claims to feel that 5 percent would be appropriate—five times more than the government actually spends.[27]

In cultivating the mistaken belief that politicians and

bureaucrats are undisciplined spenders draining the economy, critics have diverted attention from the real causes of, and the solutions necessary, to remedy shortages of opportunity. They have also fostered an illusion that improvements in the standard of living have originated only from private market forces—from the dynamic of individual initiative, competition, and free enterprise—and that the government has not produced jobs or wealth.

Such a view may be a bit hurtful to teachers, to inspectors of our food, to policemen, to members of the military, and to many others like them. Are theirs not real, or important, or productive jobs simply because the government created and paid for most of them? Don't their jobs contribute to the nation's quality of life?

Still, the point can be made that these jobs at bottom depend upon the taxpayers' ability to support them, and that the taxpayers' ability to do so depends upon income generated in the private economy. According to this line of argument, everything ultimately derives from the wealth creation of the private sector.

But what have the great advances in the private sector themselves depended upon? I am not referring here to the government's legal protection of property rights, an obvious key to the successful functioning of a free market, or to the government's role in creating the economy's infrastructure or in educating the workforce. The computer, jet air transport, the communications revolution that space satellites made possible, penicillin, and television—all vital to today's material standard of living—each became possible (or was greatly hastened) by substantial government funding for research and investment. In many of these cases, the government itself provided the market for the products until they could be produced cheaply enough for a private market to develop and prosper.[28] The greater the financial risk and the longer the time horizon before any profits can be realized, the more unlikely is the private sector to be an unaided generator of fundamental economic advance, and the more essential is governmental involvement in funding part or all of the up-front investment costs of the industry, or in providing the initial markets for products.

Monopolies, legalized and then regulated by government, sometimes serve as an alternative means of overcoming the inhibitions and other limitations of a competitive private market. The development of the first microchips took place thanks to a government-protected monopoly.[29] For a number of reasons, both telephone and electric and gas services originated and matured as monopolies, legalized and regulated by government. So did the road and highway system, an obvious precondition for the expansion of the automobile industry.

In 1940 barely 40 percent of American families owned their own homes; by 1960 half again as many American families (62 percent) had become homeowners, in no small part thanks to the GI Bill of Rights, the financing of home loans at low interest rates by the Veterans Administration and Federal Housing Administration, and tax-supported interest deductions on home mortgages. The development of suburban living as a genuine alternative to urban living was the result of government financing of highways and homeownership, in partnership with the private sector. In one manner or another, many of the elements that define today's material standard of living have required substantial initiative and activism on the part of the government and a close collaboration between government and the private sector. In a larger number of instances than many people recognize, government has been a silent partner—a kind of "invisible hand"—creating and nurturing economic developments we are apt to assume grew solely out of the competitive forces of the private market.

Running in 1995 for the Republican presidential nomination, former Tennessee governor Lamar Alexander characterized the federal government in his stump speeches as "the arrogant empire" loosely comparable to the "evil empire" that once was the Soviet Union. "One down and one to go," was his message to the cheering crowds.[30] Yet the conviction that a government "very deeply out of control," in Speaker Newt Gingrich's words, accounts for much of the economic pain afflicting American households today fails to acknowledge that it is not a poorly performing economy which has given rise to the scarcity of adequate jobs, that government maintains a lower profile in this country than in virtually any other nation on earth, and that the expansion of government's general revenue programs as well as its regulations over the past thirty years has remained steadfastly proportional to the growth of the economy as a whole. It also ignores the vital role the government has played and must play in the incubation and nurturing of private economic activities and their translation into new economic opportunity and the advancement of material well-being—a role well understood by the nation's founders, both those who gave birth to the nation in the latter half of the eighteenth century and those who reunified and were responsible for its rebirth in the middle of the nineteenth century.

Government is the mechanism by which the community as a body is represented and acts as a collectivity. No other such mechanism exists. To argue that the operations of government are naturally ineffective, wasteful, and counterproductive is to say that the community cannot act as a collective body to address legitimate claims of suffering and pain from its individual citizens; it is to rationalize inaction in the name of good public policy.

RECAPTURING THE AMERICAN ETHOS

Trying to find its moral compass and regain its sense of well-being and security, America today stands at a crossroads. That people should be able to take control over their lives, that there ought to be a place for all people of good character—this ethos has been integral to American thinking about the requirements of a good and secure society from the time of the founders. Americans place a high value on moral character. It is the foundation for everything else. The work ethic and its associated virtues of industriousness, self-discipline, perseverance, and personal responsibility are supposed to be moral anchors in our lives. To the degree that the opportunity to make a living considered minimally decent by society and to advance is unavailable to many of those who practice these virtues, however, the virtues themselves weaken and lose their grip. As with anything else, the work ethic is more likely to thrive in people's lives if it actually pays off. Surely we would not expect these virtues to gain strength if, in the experience of a large number of Americans, they led nowhere.

Historian Gertrude Himmelfarb reminds us that the thinkers who shaped the nation all "believed in the intimate relation between the character of the people and the health of the polity."[1] Virtue, she observed, was once the critical defining attribute of the good life and the good society.[2] Certainly no one-to-one relationship exists between the scarcity of economic opportunity and societal problems such as welfare dependency, family dissolution, teenage illegitimacy, and crime and juvenile delinquency, yet each of these problems clearly has an economic dimension.[3] How can successful answers to any of them be found in the absence, for tens of millions of people, of the opportunity to earn a minimally decent livelihood and get ahead by way of practicing the work ethic? Martin Luther King, Jr., paraphrasing Madison, was right to say: "There is nothing more dangerous than to build a society with a large segment of people in that society who feel they have no stake in it, who feel that they have nothing to lose."[4] We have been moving dangerously closer to becoming just such a society.

The American ethos sets up the expectation that human dignity and the ability to earn a decent living are intimately connected. It is not surprising, as a result, that the dearth of jobs that provide a decent living (not simply the absolute lack of jobs) would be deeply demoralizing in the eyes of workers. When Peter Uberroth, then chair of the Rebuild L.A. program, claimed in 1993 that "minimum wage jobs bring dignity to those who labor in them,"[5] workers organized a protest in front of his office. Some might blame envy and resentment of those better off for the indignant workers' response. But surely these workers, in the absence of better-paying jobs and with firsthand knowledge of the impossibility of maintaining families on low-wage work—and living in a society where the principle of equal moral worth has importance and where providing a decent liveli-hood is a measure of basic respect and acceptance—were react-ing to a real injustice.

For all these reasons America professes to believe that the mark of a good society is the availability of genuine opportunity to all its citizens. All elements of the political spectrum, from one end to the other, agree that "the moral society is one that allows all its citizens—and not just its upper-class ones—to lead decent lives."[6] America tells its citizens that opportunity to make a decent living exists for anyone willing to work and to persevere. Yet, for many Americans, the incantation is untrue. How long can they go on blaming themselves? Indeed, how long can we ask them to blame themselves and to take responsibility for cir-cumstances largely outside their control? "The core of being an American is the ethic of personal responsibility," Speaker of the House Newt Gingrich correctly points out.[7] The core of being an American is under terrific siege today, but from a different direction than Speaker Gingrich and others would have us believe. Personal responsibility without opportunity is a contra-diction in terms.

Conventional wisdom today has it that the free market—the private sector—contains the dynamic power that could gen-erate the necessary opportunity if we would only remove some of the myriad governmental restraints shackling the economy. But the American economy is *already* one of the least restrained in the world,[8] job creation has been strong, and a fair amount of the innovative dynamism and employment success the private sector has demonstrated in this country during the past half century was itself assisted by a variety of collaborative interventions of government.[9] Moreover, even if the economy were to generate jobs at superior rates, and if it were able to do so year after year continuously without a single business downturn, the massive shortage of adequate opportunity would still take more than a generation to overcome.[10] Claims that an unrestricted and unaided private sector can do the job effectively are simplistic.

Nor does the free market provide sufficient answer to the question of how best to sustain the values that America has stood for from the beginning. Within the free market, individual human beings are economically expendable. The individual's labor has value; not his or her character and moral agency. People who happen to be severely handicapped or ill, or are very slow learners, or who happen to face conditions of a substantial surplus of labor as compared to available jobs may find themselves unable to find gainful work or work providing wages able to sustain a family decently, enabling them to attain competency and independence or to advance, regardless of their good character. No matter how honest, dedicated, or in other ways virtuous, people will be left out according to the impersonal laws of supply and demand. We as a nation may care that this is so; the excluded individuals may care; the free market does not. A society based on the equal moral worth of each individual would give priority to the notion of making a decent place for each individual willing to work hard and persevere; this priority has no such standing in a free market.

For all of these reasons, the American ethos is not—and has never been—fully synonymous with the idea of the free market or free enterprise. However, this does not mean that the free market can't be an important part of the answer. No other major economy in the world can match the success the United States economy has had as a job creator. We ought not to ignore the role played by government in the effectiveness of the private sector, but neither should we overlook the power of the private sector or as an absolutely vital source of innovation and energy appropriately supported and regulated by government.

An alternative to the American experience is the Western European model, the social welfare state, built upon substantially larger governmental assistance programs. Rates of poverty are low in most of these economies, certainly when compared to the situation in the United States. In the case of those who are employed in Europe, wages for both the bottom fifth of workers and the average worker are generally higher, relative to the top fifth of workers, than occurs in this country. At the same time, the job creation potential of these economies has been notably low. The economies of Germany, France, Sweden, and Italy have generated few net new jobs for more than two decades now. In some of these countries, unemployment assistance amounts to nearly double what it is in the United States and the assistance extends far longer than it does here. Low job creation coupled with generous unemployment and other social welfare benefits mean that the proportion of eighteen-to-sixty-four-year-olds employed in these countries, adjusted for hours of employment, has fallen by nearly one fifth since 1973.[11] Even as poverty is low, unemployment is comparatively high. The expense to the state and to both the business and individual taxpayers of paying people not to work has become so costly and burdensome that most of the countries are in the process of scaling back their social benefits significantly. The European welfare state, like the American approach, fails to provide an effective answer.

We must direct our sights to a fresh model, a new paradigm: a society that offers genuine incentive to engage in productive work, a society where the opportunity to work exists for all, a society where all who do work receive an adequate return. We seek a society that makes a decent life possible for all, not through welfare, but by providing the opportunity needed to attain competency and independence through practicing the work ethic and to advance by improving one's work. This is the true American Dream, the vision of the nation that inspired founders such as Jefferson, Madison, and Franklin, the vision of America that Lincoln reaffirmed.

The nation's founders never saw competency and independence in terms that were strictly individualistic, as applying simply to the isolated or atomistic individual. In their eyes, the independent unit was the household or family. Competency and independence were meant to enable families to form and to thrive. Moreover, most of the founders believed that individuals and families would—and should—enjoy a still fuller social life by forming larger communities of mutually supportive people. Within a larger community, others were there to help when illness struck, crops needed harvesting, or a new building had to be erected, or when there were hard times. Competency and independence would undergird a rich community life, not be its contrary; the world of independent citizens the founders had in mind was a strongly social one. Therefore, the amount of work needed to attain independence was not expected to require so much time and energy as to monopolize an individual's efforts, but would leave individuals time to get meaningfully involved both in the life of their family and in the life of their community.[12]

It might be said that in considering the expenditure of resources it requires, this ethos of economic independence and advancement based upon work and perseverance must ultimately run up against natural environmental limits. However, competency and independence do not demand or even necessarily encourage lavish lifestyles. They are entirely compatable with modest living standards. They do not suggest material reward as the sole object of life, either: the ethos is highly attentive to the incorporation of full and rich family and community involvement into everyday life. Moreover, material advancement based on improved performance does not always dictate greater consumption of resources. On the contrary, if it improves the efficiency of resource use, advancement through gains in worker performance could end up placing little added demand on resources.

If we are going to fashion a nation that provides opportunity for economic independence and advancement based on practicing the work ethic, what can be done? The proposals I will suggest are meant to spur discussion, not end it. Though comprising a comprehensive whole, they are made up of individual parts that are independent of each other. One does not depend upon another. Rather than being started all at once, any one of them can be put in place on its own without having to act on the others. There may be other meritorious proposals that deserve our attention, too, possibly more so than the ones I offer. Experimentation and testing with pilot projects is possible as well. What is not acceptable is to take *no* action. Failure to act, in the face of what the evidence of this book documents, would amount to nothing less than a denunciation of the seminal creed that the nation claims to follow.

Recapturing the vision of the American ethos requires first that we have measures capable of telling whether we are moving closer to or further away from the objectives. Measures of the economy's performance used today—the gross national product (GNP), unemployment, and inflation—are confusing and misleading. According to each of these standard measures, the economy thrived from 1979 to 1989: the real GNP rose by 27 percent, from $3.8 trillion to $4.8 trillion (in 1987 dollars); on a per person basis, the GNP after inflation rose by 16 percent; unemployment fell from 5.8 to 5.2 percent; and inflation eased from 13.5 to 4.6 percent. All the same, the nation moved further away from the basic precepts of the American ethos, not closer to them. During those very same years, the shortfall in adequate jobs mounted, growing from 8 million in 1979 to beyond 15 million in 1989, while the percentage shortfall in adequate jobs as compared to households in need of such jobs rose by almost half, from 16 percent to 23 percent. At 23 percent, the opportunity deficit in 1989 stood four times higher than the unemployment rate. Apart from those who were unable to reach a base-line wage, nearly two fifths of American households working year-round full-time experienced a real decline in their hourly wage over the decade.

The GNP, the unemployment rate, the rate of inflation, and other similar indicators do not directly measure what should be the primary goal of our economy: the welfare of households. The rate at which adequate economic opportunity is available to households—if we compare the total number of adequate job opportunities present in the economy to the total number of households whose living depends upon employment, adjusting for supplemental earners—is a far more revealing yardstick than today's standard indicators. Such measures also need to examine wage and salary advancement—the proportion of workers providing able to advance in real hourly pay over a defined period of time. An even simpler measure would focus on the number of distressed workers and the proportion they comprise of the total labor force, defining as distressed those workers who experience any one of the following three conditions: they work year-round full-time but receive pay that falls below an adequate hourly wage; they are employed part-time because they have been unable to find full-time work; or they have been unemployed for longer than twenty-six weeks and are looking for work. From

1979 to 1989, while the real GNP rose and the unemployment rate declined, the number of distressed workers increased from about 11.7 million to just over 20 million; the proportion of the labor force consisting of distressed workers climbed from 11.1 percent to 16.7 percent.[13] The economy was moving forward according to the usual indicators but backwards according to indicators of economic opportunity. The whole nature and direction of the national debate concerning the quality of our economic lives would be very different were it rooted in indicators that directly measure the reality of economic conditions facing American households.

A long lineup of mistaken solutions must also be discarded if we are to act effectively on our national aspirations and bring a vision based on the American ethos to realization. Most politicians and a large segment of the public look to economic growth as the answer. Something is the matter, though, when annual rates of the economy's overall growth fairly close to those of Great Britain at the apogee of the industrial revolution, as ours have been since 1973, are viewed as inadequate.[14] I will momentarily suggest ways to improve the economy's growth, but the economy's growth is not the main problem. Indeed, *no amount of expansion by the economy will suffice if improvements in the productivity of workers remain only weakly reflected in overall hourly compensation, and if such compensation growth as workers do receive continues to be channeled primarily to the upper fifth of workers.* As observed in Chapter 6, these two factors alone built up over the years so that by 1994 they rechaneled more than $400 billion in compensation annually away from the lower 80 percent of the labor force. Rethinking the level of overall growth in the economy that we should consider satisfactory comprises part of the redefinition of economic performance and its proper measurement which needs to get under way.

It is crucial, too, to get beyond conventional solutions based on false beliefs about what has caused the alleged slow growth of the nation's economy and hence the constriction of opportunity. Neither governmental intrusiveness nor the challenge of global competition is a primary source of the decline in opportunity facing American households.[15] Nor is an alleged decline in investment.[16] Proposals that would gut taxes, governmental programs, and regulations in the name of igniting business activity and economic growth, or that would raise trade protections in the name of establishing a level global playing field, will do little to provide true solutions. Like the standard measures of the economy and the claims of slow economic growth, these shibboleths cloud the debate and divert attention from the real issues.

To be effective, solutions must address the real causes: the disconnect between the wage growth of workers and their productivity improvement; the increasing redirection of the wage growth to the top fifth of workers; and the slowdown in the overall productivity improvement among workers itself.

The first two of these—the disconnects between wage growth and productivity and the redirection of wage growth to the top fifth of earners—are apt to occur under conditions where an imbalance exists in the relations between employers and workers. Since the 1960s organized workers have declined from 31 percent of the labor force to 13 percent today. While opponents of worker organization say that unions are responsible for the decline of the American economy, and with it the stagnating levels of real compensation, the fact is that stalled compensation levels in the United States since 1973 have coincided with labor's loss of power. Nor do we have, as some suggest, an overpaid unionized workforce unable to face stiff global competition. Compensation of workers from rival industrialized countries such as Germany, who generally compete successfully in world trade with overall productivity not superior to our own, gained parity with the compensation of American workers and began to surpass it nearly two decades ago. Comparing different nations, economist Richard Freeman found that the spread of earnings inequality within a nation was inversely related to the proportion of organized workers in the economy. Earnings inequality became sharpest, Freeman discovered, in economies with relatively low and declining union membership.[17] The connection between wage growth and productivity growth has been closest, too, only in nations in which organized workers have a strong presence.[18] The wages of American workers who are not organized fall short of those of organized workers by 26 percent on average, and by a whopping 56 percent in the case of blue-collar jobs.[19] When workers both are poorly organized and have few alternative job opportunities, their ability to attain higher wages that match productivity is gravely weakened. This has increasingly been the case in the United States since the 1960s.

In the minds of the founders, workers having little or no control over their work was antithetical to the idea of independence. Strengthening worker organization—not necessarily in the old adversarial, centralized style many unions grew into but according to far more team-based, participatory, and collaborative models suited to a post-industrial economy[20]—can help improve both the productivity and wage picture of the average American household. When labor held a more equal bargaining position, the size of overall wage advances kept pace with the size of overall productivity growth, and wage advances were more equitably distributed to benefit the average worker. As a consequence, the large majority of workers found that their wages improved over time. Strengthened worker participation can enable private-sector forces to begin to redress the growing gap between workers' wages and their productivity and the increasing inequality of wages among the workers themselves.

The creation of a sufficient supply of jobs to match the level of need is a different matter, however. More effective worker participation can do little to generate new jobs or ensure that enough adequate jobs will come into being for the numbers of workers in want of them. Overwhelming demographic forces coupled with powerful cultural developments can still leave gapping shortages of opportunity, such as the present one of nearly 16 million adequate jobs, that stronger worker participation by itself cannot do much to address.

Government, building upon the private economy at every turn, must be involved in addressing the enormous deficit that exists in the availability of adequate jobs. A comprehensive set of governmental actions that would generate a sufficient supply of solid adequate jobs, created primarily by and through the private sector, would require approximately $110 billion a year—after subtracting the reduced costs that would accrue to the current public assistance programs. This figure includes the cost of providing adequate child care and health insurance to full-time working households that lack coverage. An additional $70 billion will be needed to provide the educational and training boost necessary to spur productivity improvements closer to the levels achieved over the years 1945–65.

In designing an approach to eliminate the shortage of nearly 16 million adequate jobs, it is important to take into account that many steady year-round full-time jobs presently exist that do not pay an adequate wage or offer adequate health coverage. Since the jobs already exist, they do not have to be created anew. About 7 million heads of households now occupy such jobs. The pay of these jobs needs to be brought to an adequate level—to a wage of $7.60 per hour or more in 1994 dollars—and supplemented with health coverage if these jobs are to be considered adequate. The minimum wage can do part of the work. By 1998 the minimum wage will be at about $4.65 per hour in 1994 dollars. It should be raised modestly (by less than 15 percent), reset at $5.25 per hour ($5.90 in 1998 dollars), and then indexed at that level so that it does not fall below 47 percent of the average wage of nonsupervisory workers, approximately its relative size during most of the 1950s.[21]

The earned income tax credit (EITC) can lift the pay of these 7 million jobs the rest of the way up to an adequate wage. The EITC acts as a credit on income tax. Available to low-wage employed workers, the credit operates to raise household income. The size of the credit depends on the level of earned income of the household. The EITC is capable of providing base-line earnings to all households with year-round full-time workers. Because it is refundable, whenever the credit exceeds the tax owed by the household, the household then receives a payment for that amount from the government so that the credit becomes a form of wage subsidy for workers in low-wage jobs. The size of the subsidy can be set to make up the difference between the minimum wage earnings for a year-round full-time worker and an adequate wage for households whose total income falls below a base-line income. To do so, with the new minimum wage, the total size of the credit at its maximum would need to increase from $3,400 a year to $4,700.[22] As it does now, the credit would thereafter decline as household income increased until the credit dropped to zero.[23] The resulting credit in combination with the new minimum wage would underpin the transformation of all existing year-round full-time jobs into jobs offering an adequate wage.

Of course, apart from these 7 million existing jobs, many more jobs are needed. Somewhere around an additional 11 million new year-round full-time jobs paying adequate wages are required, assuming that about one fifth of the added jobs go to new supplemental earners. Some of these added jobs will come about by natural means through the economy's normal growth. If the economy generates added jobs at the same healthy rate it has since 1973 (about 2 percent a year),[24] the net surplus of adequate jobs as compared to the number of new workers entering into the labor force will be about 500,000 a year.[25] If we can depend on past growth rates and projected demographic changes, that is, we can expect surpluses arising from the normal job growth of the economy to do part of the work, to the tune of a cumulative 5 million adequate jobs over 10 years, leaving the gap to be filled at around 6 million adequate jobs.

Two routes exist to generate these 6 million needed new jobs: the private sector and the public sector. As much as possible, new job creation ought to be carried out through the private sector. To try to intensify job creation through the private sector, the government can offer subsidies to private businesses that will create new jobs above and beyond normal levels. Some years ago, in 1977–78, an experimental program known as the new jobs tax credit (NJTC) subsidized half of the first $10,000 in wages (in 1994 dollars) paid to up to fifty workers that a business hired above 102 percent of the previous year's employment level. A condition that the jobs be year-round full-time could be added, and even that the jobs pay greater than some base level, say $6.25 per hour. The trigger of 102 percent could also be adjusted slightly upward in order to ensure that the new jobs are beyond normal growth. The Treasury Department failed to publicize the program, yet economists Robert Haveman and John Schloz of the University of Wisconsin Institute for Research on Poverty report that "research evaluations indicate that it was successful in creating jobs . . . and at a rather low cost to the Treasury. Up to

30 percent of the 1977–78 employment growth in the studied industries was attributable to the program." In all industries across the entire economy during those two years, including those untouched by the program, 7.3 million new jobs were created. Haveman and Schloz added that a new NJTC program should raise the cap of fifty new hires so as to give greater incentive to large firms to utilize the program.[26]

Additional approaches that utilize the private sector could direct government spending more in ways that favor firms which increase jobs and base pay rapidly.[27] Incentives can also reduce taxes on firms that apply profits toward the generation of greater numbers of adequate jobs. We presently provide tax incentives to spur the use of profits for investment. Why not grant tax incentives that, in addition, spur the use of profits for the creation of more adequate jobs?

The objective should be to generate at least 75 percent of the new jobs by way of various incentives directed to the private sector. If this goal were met, 4.5 million new jobs would be created over a ten-year period through private-sector incentives of one kind or another at a cost of approximately $33 billion annually. In addition, the EITC assistance for these workers—as well as for the workers occupying low-wage jobs already in existence and for workers at higher wages as the credit is phased out—will cost about $31 billion annually beyond current spending.

Public jobs comprise still another approach. Although secondary, they remain a necessary component of an employment creation strategy unless the private sector proves able, through natural means, to generate job creation considerably in excess of the 5 million surplus expected from the normal yearly increase. The need for public service workers ranges widely and includes, among others, rehabilitating housing and bringing it up to present-day codes, supervising playgrounds, parks, and city neighborhoods to promote safety and reduce crime, enhancing child and health care services, aiding teachers with routine administrative activities and assisting with discipline, helping keep streets and neighborhoods clean, and extending the hours of libraries and other public facilities, including in the evenings and weekends. The city of Milwaukee found in 1993 that it had unmet needs in the public arena estimated at more than 50,000 jobs, which amounted to greater than 5 percent of the area's total employment.[28] Job creation nationally, on the scale of unmet needs discovered in Milwaukee, would far surpass the required 1.5 million year-round full-time public jobs. Were 1.5 million public jobs fashioned, the cost would amount to about $26 billion annually, including the EITC necessary to bring the minimum wage these jobs would offer up to an adequate wage and job search funds to help move the workers over time from public- into private-sector employment.

One consideration related to these and other jobs concerns the situation faced by single parents. Calculation of an adequate hourly wage for a family with one or two children assumes that two adults in the household are employed, an assumption that applies rather differently in the cases of many single-parent families. True, in these cases year-round full-time employment combined with child support from the absent parent ought to suffice. However, frequently the absent parent pays no child support, or pays far too little to provide satisfactorily for the household even when added to the single parent's year-round full-time earnings. The government has become far more diligent in recent years in this area, but it can do nothing if the absent parent is unemployed or if the court itself has awarded inadequate child support. The government should continue its intensified vigilance and enforcement of child-support payments. It ought to push courts to raise these payments, wherever feasible, to no less than

$2,500 a year per child. Where this alternative is not feasible,[29] the government ought to assure full-time employed single parents[30] living on incomes less than $16,000 child support of no less than $2,000 per child (including absent-parent support) for up to two children. The net cost (above and beyond court-awarded payments from the absent parents) would amount to about $26 billion.[31] Implementation of such a program would provide the government with increased incentive to retrieve as much of the cost as possible from the absent parents. Would such a guarantee also give low-income families with children an incentive to dissolve in the hope of obtaining an additional $2,000 to $4,000 from the government? It would not seem likely given that the absent parent would still be liable for support and that a condition of payment would be that the remaining single parent be employed full-time.[32]

A final consideration has to do with the adequacy of health care. In the present American health care system, a great number of low-wage working households have no insurance. The large majority of workers employed at the average wage or above have access to medical insurance connected with their employment. Moreover, welfare recipients are covered under Medicaid, and older Americans receive Medicare. By contrast, as many as one third to one half of workers paid wages up to $7.60 an hour have no medical insurance attached to their jobs. Households with no access to health insurance cannot be said to be truly independent. Providing coverage for these workers is a complicated matter, however. Complications arise not simply because of the cost, which would total somewhere around $35 billion annually beyond current spending, assuming each individual household that would benefit also contributes up to $2,000 a year, including all co-payments.[33] The more serious complication has to do with how to keep businesses and employees from "free-riding." Once businesses know that subsidized health coverage to uninsured workers is available, at least some of them will abandon their own insurance schemes. Their workers, then uncovered, would seek individual coverage now made less costly to both the workers and the businesses by virtue of the government's subsidy. The estimated cost to taxpayers will grow substantially if companies act in this manner. Some structural changes thus must take place in the American health care system to assure coverage of uninsured workers without creating this result. Once structural solutions have been agreed upon, the cost of covering uninsured workers beyond present spending and payments by the affected households will amount to approximately $35 billion.

Such insurance, and its price, would include the cost of coverage for households during periods of job loss and unemployment. A similar program, paid for privately in mortgage or rent payments, could easily be made available to families to cover part or all of the cost of housing when job dislocations have occurred, reducing the fear during a time of exceptional stress that one could lose one's home.

All the costs taken together to ensure job adequacy amount to $155 billion. Yet, once fully implemented, these actions should make welfare programs—present public assistance, food stamps, housing subsidies, and child nutrition—largely redundant except in cases where transitional assistance is needed.

As more adequate jobs capable of supporting a family become available to adults on welfare, more household heads will find opportunities and incentives to take and keep jobs. Moreover, if adequate jobs are available and welfare recipients fail to seek or take work after a transitional period, we might then be ready to follow through on the idea of terminating welfare and allowing private charities to take up the task of helping these households deal with their circumstances—a stance we cannot and should not take until we have assurances that sufficient opportunities actually do exist for hardworking people to attain a decent livelihood through their own labor.

Of the present costs of these programs, up to 75 percent of the $80 billion now spent annually is directed to continuing rather than transitional assistance; these costs can be reduced and folded into the new programs. If 60 percent of the expenditures under the present welfare system are cut, the net cost of the new programs will be about $110 billion.

While these measures hope to create enough adequate jobs so that everyone willing to work hard and persevere can make a decent living, they do not address the issue of the ability of households to improve their productivity, and to keep moving ahead by doing so. Recall that the educational advance of Americans increased by barely 5 percent between 1970 and 1990 (from 12.1 years to 12.7 years) as compared to a 30 percent advance that took place in the twenty years from 1950 to 1970 (from 9.3 years to 12.1 years).[34] Many observers attribute the slowdown in productivity improvement by American workers since 1970 to a slackening of investment, yet no reduction in investment occurred. Business net investment remained the same proportion of the GNP during both the decade before and after 1970.[35] But the educational advance of Americans decelerated sharply after 1970.

In its growth and development since 1970, the American educational system has left one half of the population out in the cold. Many people lack the scholastic aptitude, financial resources, or even the natural inclination to go to college—about half of American adults have gotten no education beyond high school. For those now left out, the nation badly needs to establish a full-scale, intellectually demanding apprenticeship program, one that couples *both* academics and job skills.[36] Such a program would enroll high school students, say, in their last three semesters of high school, and for three semesters beyond high school. By combining in-class academic and skills education along with on-site training and skills application, the programs would prepare students who do not want to go on to college to meet the demands of the contemporary economy. In the words of economists Eileen Appelbaum and Rosemary Batt, "The broad skills in apprenticeship programs completed by most German frontline workers enables managers to assign workers to various tasks, as needed, and workers to master new skills more easily."[37] The result is higher-quality production by workers trained to develop sufficient flexibility along with cutting-edge technical skills so as to be able to adapt quickly and effectively to changing market conditions. At the same time, programs are needed to enhance the skills and productivity of middle-aged workers and dislocated workers of all ages in ways suited to contemporary market requirements. The programs must not simply be affordable and effective but also provide some financial aid to help workers and their families get by during retraining.

Were the nation to develop comprehensive school-to-work apprenticeship programs for late teenage and young adult students adapted from the German model, the net cost would come to somewhere around $25 billion a year. The cost assumes that 40 percent of all students in the twelfth grade and second half of the eleventh grade elected to enter a three-year program, and subtracts the costs high schools presently bear for these students. A high-quality retraining program, particularly for workers in their middle years who have been displaced, would cost another net $25 billion yearly. Such a program should cover 2.5 million workers each year with maximum assistance of $15,000 for each worker for tuition and help with living expenses. Unemployment benefits and present training measures for these workers would be folded into the program. Assisting 2.5 million workers yearly would accommodate virtually all workers whose jobs are lost each year and so become dislocated. Present assistance programs accommodate about 500,000 such workers a year, and they afford most of these workers a far lesser level of support. Added to the net expense of $110 billion for the measures designed to generate adequate jobs, the package of programs needed not simply to create sufficient jobs but also to enable larger numbers of workers to improve the level of their skills and productivity comes to a net cost of $160 billion annually.

Even more can be done to secure ultimate productivity improvements through educational attainment if we are willing to begin before further education, at the grade school level. *All* students need better preparation prior to further education, which in turn will enhance their learning at that level. Greater individual attention in grade school and high school is vital to providing better preparation, an objective complicated by the imminent rise in the number of students. Yet widespread agreement exists that reducing the size of classes is among the most important actions that can be taken to improve educational outcomes, both in terms of educational achievement and the desire to advance one's education. California has established an incentive program of voluntary collaboration between the state, local school districts, and individual schools designed to bring about and finance reductions of class sizes to fewer than twenty students. Based on the costs it is projecting, reducing class sizes for every public school student in the nation through sixth grade, including the provision of new infrastructure, would cost slightly more than $20 billion a year above present expenditures. The net cost of the total package of programs comes to about $180 billion yearly.

We can expect these actions on the educational front to boost productivity and to do so ever more significantly over the years. In turn, the productivity improvements will find their way into pay raises more effectively as the relations between workers and employers gain greater balance. Indeed, increased worker participation is apt to improve productivity on its own, since the role employees play in the workplace influences the productivity success of workers. Economists have found the level of performance of workers to be significantly related to a real, rather than merely consultative, participatory voice for labor; to protection of the rights of workers; and to profit sharing.[38] In addition, effective works councils aid in the flow of information and in the dissemination of new ideas and practices.[39] Correctly done, economist David Levine observes, employee participation contributes significantly to improved productivity, a conclusion that research strongly supports.[40]

Getting the nation back on track so that full-time employment delivers a decent living and enables households to advance through improved performance has a high price attached to it. A tax bill of about $180 billion is substantial—and so are its attendant political costs.

As a proportion of all personal income (excluding all transfer payments), the needed $180 billion in revenues comes to an additional four cents on the dollar, not a small amount but also not exorbitant given the many profound issue at stake. If the issue came to be viewed as one that the entire community ought to address, the cost would spread among all taxpayers and would still leave American taxpayers paying among the lowest taxes in the industrialized world. At the other end of the spectrum, the nation could call especially upon the direct beneficiaries of the market redistribution of earnings—the top fifth, and especially the top tenth, of earners. A tax of less than 1 percent on the household wealth of the top tenth of households would net more than $90 billion annually.[41] Placing Social Security taxation on half of individual earnings above $65,000 a year would raise approximately another $55 billion.[42] Eliminating tax write-offs for high-income households, such as for mortgage interest payments totaling more than $50,000 yearly for one or more houses, and other similar tax preferences, would bring in an additional $25 billion a year. These taxes, once more, would leave top-income groups of Americans still paying among the lowest taxes in the industrialized world. Since they will gain from such programs, corporations and businesses surely could pay one fourth (approximately $12 billion a year) of the costs of the apprenticeship and retraining initiatives. Together, these sources would bring in $180 billion annually. The workers assisted by the retraining programs could also be asked to repay a portion of the assistance over time. Moreover, the increased productivity created by the measures for basic education, apprenticeship, and retraining will ultimately add still more tax revenues to the government, by way of increased wage earnings and business profits.

Alternatively, inestimable costs are entailed by leaving millions of Americans marginalized and tolerating the inability of so many more to improve their living standard. It is not only the price paid in addressing problems of dependency, illegitimacy, crime, and other serious social dysfunctions, or the cumulating costs resulting from an erosion of the work ethic or from lessened productivity, but also the very high toll that the diminished sense of economic security and well-being takes on much of the citizenry.

It is said that we live in an age that opposes collective societal decisions, an age of vastly lowered expectations of government. It is worth noting, at the same time, that more than two-thirds of the public believes the nation's government is a vehicle capable of making ours a better country. Many more members of the public look to the government in this regard than to the private sector and either large corporations or small businesses. As we observed in Chapter 8, the government indeed has been not only more effective but also far more disciplined than is commonly portrayed.

Ever since the nation's beginnings, the concepts of "freedom," "personal responsibility," and "self-discipline" have resonated deeply for Americans. So has the idea of "opportunity." Opportunity holds such a vital place that leading spokespersons on the right, not to mention the left, quickly acknowledge that individuals deserve help and assistance when they have little or no opportunity.[43] True choice exists, personal accountability can be realized, and self-discipline and the work ethic can thrive only in the presence of opportunity. Yet the truth of the matter is that an immense shortage of opportunity to earn a decent living and move ahead permeates the nation and has done so for the past thirty years or longer. The shortage has a magnitude far greater than anyone has imagined. The entire foundation of the nation has been weak since the 1950s. The situation bears some analogy to a game of musical chairs in which a larger number of contestants fight over a lesser number of seats—only this game involves millions rather than a handful of people who have been closed out and it concerns the most basic conditions shaping their lives. Exacerbating a series of social pathologies, the grave shortage of opportunity confounds the realization of the precepts held by the nation's founders as to what is necessary to sustain a stable and secure republican society. It contradicts the nation's deepest moral understandings about right and wrong. It corrodes the spirit of the nation and undermines the effectiveness of its public policies. It turns us against one another. That there be genuine opportunity for everyone—along with the commitment to share necessary to ensure the availability of opportunity to everyone—is a worthy and a demanding moral ideal, an ideal that stands at the heart of the proposition to which the nation is dedicated. It is against this moral ideal that we must measure ourselves.

APPENDIX A

The economy contains a greater number of openings at any single point in time than employment figures indicate. The figures do not include a number of sources of job openings. For example, job openings that never get filled do not register in the employment statistics. In addition, the potential that exists for self-employment by which enterprising individuals create their own jobs and sustain their own living does not register in the employment statistics, either.

A true picture of the number of jobs existing in the economy must include the openings that have been on offer but never get filled and so ultimately die. They are sometimes called "depressed openings." The analysis contained in the book takes these jobs into account; but since they are rarely directly measured, the analysis must do so by way of making estimates. The procedure I use starts by making an estimate of the total number of job vacancies (the total includes both eventually filled and depressed or never-filled vacancies) from the unemployment statistics. I then derive the number of depressed or never-filled vacancies from the estimate of total vacancies. Both the estimate of total job vacancies and the derivation of the number of never-filled vacancies build upon the work of the economist Katharine Abraham.[1]

The results of her investigation of job vacancies found that the job vacancy rate was related to the unemployment rate. Her estimates indicated that the rate of unemployment in January 1978 of 7.0 percent coincided with an unemployment–job vacancy ratio of 7.5 to 1 (meaning that there were 7.5 people unemployed for every vacant job); in contrast, the 4.0 percent unemployment rate of January 1968 coincided with an unemployment–job vacancy ratio of 1.3 to 1. The mean number of days that job vacancies lasted in 1978, she estimated, came to 5, and to 15 in 1968. It is reasonable to conclude that never-filled vacancies lasted considerably longer than vacancies that became filled, however, perhaps as long as one to three months or more. A set of surveys cited by Abraham suggests that never-filled job vacancies likely total no more than 6 percent of all vacancies at any point in time.[2] However, since never-filled vacancies have a life duration that extends five to six times longer than filled vacancies,[3] over the span of a year never-filled vacancies will amount to no more than about 1 percent of all job vacancies. If the unemployment–job vacancy ratio is 7.5 to 1, as in January 1978, and a total of 6.2 million workers were unemployed, then the total number of vacancies during the five-day mean period would have been 830,000,[4] or 60.5 million job vacancies during the whole year.[5] If never-filled vacancies total 1 percent of all job vacancies, then never-filled vacancies would amount to approximately 605,000 in 1978.

Abraham examined periods of one month. I have just indicated how her figures might look were they yearlong instead of only for the month of January. By the same token, yearlong unemployment figures for years that Abraham did not examine can be translated into job vacancy figures for those years if we assume two things: (1) that the yearlong unemployment figure approximates the average rate of unemployment typically during the year, and (2) that the unemployment–job vacancy ratio corresponding to the unemployment rate cited for the year she examined applies reasonably consistently to a similar unemployment rate in another unexamined year. The measure for job vacancies, 1 percent of which are counted as never-filled positions, is estimated in this manner. The foundation is Abraham's unemployment–job vacancy ratio and mean duration of vacancies. I worked from the vacancy ratio and mean duration of vacancies associated with the rate of unemployment in her analysis which is closest to the unemployment rate prevailing during each of the years examined in this book.

In 1989, for example, the unemployment rate was 5.2 percent. As a result, based on Abraham's findings, the unemployment–job vacancy ratio would be about 3.3[6] and the mean duration of vacancies would be ten calendar days.[7] If 6.5 million workers were unemployed in 1989, then the total number of job vacancies for the year would be 71.9 million, and the total number of never filled job vacancies 720,000, for the year. In turn, if two thirds of the never-filled vacancies were year-round full-time jobs offering an adequate wage, then the total number of never-filled vacancies involving adequate jobs would come to 480,000 jobs. I used this procedure to estimate never-filled vacancies for 1989, and used the same procedure for each of the other years covered in the analysis.

Alongside never-filled vacancies are additional unregistered opportunities that can come by way of self-employment through new businesses. No certainty can ever exist as to how many genuine opportunities are available for enterprising people to make a living through self-employment and new incorporations. My procedure assumes that double the number of opportunities for self-employment actually exist than have been acted upon. I also assume that the success rate of these new enterprises in delivering a year-round full-time adequate wage is about 50 percent.[8] Assume further that four fifths of these enterprises endure for a median of five years and that the remaining fifth succeed for a median of twenty years. Making the calculation in this manner means that the number of persons who could be self-employed successfully in any single year is a cumulating product of what individuals could have done during prior years, sometimes many years prior. Calculating self-employment in this way and applying it to 1989 added 2.5

million employment opportunities capable of yielding adequate earnings to the job figures for 1989. Folding in the 480,000 never-filled
vacancies and adding them to the potential self-employment opportunities that were not acted upon brings the total to 2,980,000 additional year-round full-time opportunities with adequate wages that could
conceivably have been available in 1989. I added this figure of nearly 3
million adequate job opportunities to the employment figures for 1989.
In like fashion, all job availability figures cited in the book incorporate
estimates of never-filled job vacancies and self-employment job opportunities for the respective years.

APPENDIX B

Questions may arise as to the degree to which a household can be understood to be "independent" if it relies for a certain amount of its livelihood on benefit payments from the government. People may be tempted to think that independence, in the minds of the founders, requires households to make their living in a self-sufficient manner—ideally as yeomen who own their land. But the founders also considered merchants and artisans to be independent, despite the fact that each of these groups depended crucially upon the customs or demands of others to make a decent living. Thomas Jefferson believed that manufacturing workers earning wages were independent, too, as long as they genuinely had the choice of taking up occupations that provided independence through self-sufficiency in a more conventional manner. Today, we are apt to consider individuals independent if they make a decent living by working hard and if their ability to do is not dependent upon the goodwill of any single other person, such as a single employer.

Can a household be independent if the decency of its living depends partly upon other people in the form of payments from the government? Independence involves a certain character trait of individuals: a willingness and disposition to do what is necessary to earn a decent living and also to exhibit the virtues associated with earning a decent living, such as perseverance, prudence, and responsibility. The root idea behind our concern for independence is the great importance we attach to this character trait and its associated virtues. We don't want people imbued with such character and virtues to be needlessly harmed by conditions that are beyond their control. Because it operates according to the laws of supply and demand, the private market is expected to maximize efficiency. It is not set up to ensure that a necessary supply of opportunity exists so that all households willing and disposed to work hard and persevere are in fact able to make a decent living through paid employment or self-employment. For the government to step in to fill this void if a deficit of opportunity exists is analogous to what the government does—and what the public expects it to do—elsewhere in cases of market failure. Should the market fail to provide the amount of opportunity necessary to support a decent living through full-time work, it is appropriate for the government to stimulate market growth, to create jobs, and/or to regulate or supplement the wages of jobs offered through the private economy such that enough jobs become available that are capable of sustaining a decent living. If that is so, full-time working people eligible for public jobs or wage supplements as part of the income required to attain a decent living, when the private market provides no other alternative, are no less independent than are people whose wages rely wholly on the market.

APPENDIX C

An argument voiced with increasing frequency over recent years is that the growth of the American economy and the rise in wages of American workers during the past two decades have been badly understated by the government's official statistics because the government has consistently overstated inflation. This argument contends that the true rise in prices has been lower than that officially recorded by the government's Consumer Price Index, with the result that part of what the government reports as inflation is actually genuine growth. If inflation has been lower, then wage growth after adjusting for inflation would be higher than the government has reported, and analysts conclusions that the wage picture has been bleak for the past two decades would need to be reexamined.

Even if they were demonstrated to be valid, these arguments about the underestimation of inflation would have no effect on most of the results presented in this book. The analysis of the book builds upon the idea of an adequate wage, applied to 1967, 1979, and 1989.

Calculations of the adequate wage for those three years grew out of the cost of necessary items in a family budget for those years. As pointed out in Chapter 4, the prices of the items were current to each of the years. They were not and did not need to be adjusted for inflation.[1] Other relevant annual data presented in Chapter 4 that support the validity of these budgets (such as polling results concerning the public's view about the smallest income needed to get along) were also current to each of the years, not inflation-adjusted. That the deficit in adequate jobs neared 16 million in 1989, as shown in Chapter 5, or that this deficit grew by nearly half following 1979, remains so no matter what conclusions are ultimately reached regarding the rate of inflation. The same holds true for the results presented in Chapter 5 concerning mobility—the ability of workers paid less than an adequate wage to move up to an adequate wage over time. Once more, the definition and measurement of the adequate wage for any particular year were based on current prices in that year. That more than 60 percent of full-time workers starting at less than an adequate wage in 1979 were unable to move up to an adequate wage by 1989, despite consistent year-round full-time employment every year during the decade, would remain the case no matter what conclusions are reached concerning the rate of inflation for the period.

Still another component of the analysis, from Chapter 6, shows that average workers have lost hundreds of billions of dollars a year through a combination of two factors: the redirection of wages to the upper fifth of all workers and the failure of real-wage advances to keep up with productivity improvements. Calculating the former of the two factors and its effect is independent of inflation. Wage distributions are analyzed in current dollars for the year under consideration, not in inflation-adjusted dollars. Calculating the effect of the latter factor *is* influenced by the particular rate of inflation that is selected because the selection will affect how much the rise in prices over time has eroded the worth of wages. However, the discussion of the failure of real-wage advances to keep up with productivity, found in Chapter 6, has taken such issues about inflation into account. The conclusions presented in the chapter regarding the dollar effect of the differential between real-wage growth and productivity improvement hold even at lower estimates of inflation.[2]

Finally, issues about the rate of inflation could be raised regarding the real-wage advances of the average family discussed in Chapter 6. The findings indicated that the median real-wage rise for the same workers over time was 1 percent a year from 1979 to 1989; that about 42 percent of household heads gained no raise in real pay over that decade-long period; and that half of all heads of household who worked full-time either got no real-pay raise or were earning less than an adequate wage in 1989. Suppose we reject the official measures of inflation and assume instead that the government has overstated inflation by nearly one fifth. (Doing so would lead to the improbable conclusion that the American economy grew at fully as fast an annual rate from 1979 to 1989 as did the British economy during a typical decade at the height of the industrial revolution. It also assumes that the causes of the overstatement of inflation, if true, apply to low-income patterns of spending no differently than they do to average-income spending patterns.) Taking this lower rate of inflation from 1979 to 1989 as the basis for the analysis, the medial real-wage rise for the same workers during the decade would have been 1.9 percent a year, a healthy rise, although still below the 3.1 percent real-wage advances of the 1960s and early 1970s. The other effects are more modest. Thirty-four percent of household heads rather than about 42 percent, for example, would have received no raise in their real pay from 1979 to 1989. Most important, even with the depressed rate of inflation, 46 percent of all full-time working heads of household still would have failed either to get any increase in their real pay from 1979 to 1989 or to get up to an adequate wage by 1989.

NOTES

Chapter 1

1. George Will, "Two Years Later," *Washington Post*, January 19, 1995, p. A25.

2. See Calvin Trillin, "Drawing the Line," *The New Yorker*, December 12, 1994, p. 56.

3. Jennifer Hochschild, "The Political Contingency of Public Opinion, or What Shall We Make of the Declining Faith of Middle-Class African Americans?," *PS: Political Science and Politics*, vol. 27, no. 1 (March 1994): p. 36.

4. Roger Angell, "Two Dreams," *The New Yorker*, March 13, 1995, p. 7. In a certain sense the ethos recalls the powerful universal embrace that John 3:16 intends: " . . . so that everyone who believes in Him will not be lost but have real life." This common-language wording of John 3:16 is found in Robert W. Funk et al. (The Jesus Seminar), *The Five Gospels: The Search for the Authentic Words of Jesus* (New York: Macmillan, 1995), p. 408.

5. *The Federalist* (New York: Random House, Modern Library), p. 408.

6. Stephanie Fedunack, "Don't Give Up! 'Lean on Me' Principal Stresses Hard Work, Self-Reliance," *Arizona Daily Star*, October 19, 1989, p. 3B.

7. Richard Louv, "Hope in Hell's Classroom," *New York Times Magazine*, November 25, 1990, p. 75.

8. William J. Bennett, *The Moral Compass* (New York: Simon and Schuster, 1995), p. 694.

9. Ronald Reagan expressed this view, pointing out once in a speech that the Washington Sunday paper had thirty-four full pages of help wanted ads and the Los Angeles paper fifty-two such pages. See Office of the Federal Register, *U.S. Weekly Compilation of Presidential Documents*, vol. 18 (September–December 1982).

10. Tony Horwitz, "Minimum Wage Jobs Give Many Americans Only a Miserable Life," *Wall Street Journal*, November 12, 1993, p. A4.

11. Lawrence M. Mead, *The New Politics of Poverty: The Nonworking Poor in America* (New York: Basic Books, 1992), pp. 93–94.

12. *Arizona Daily Star*, April 12, 1995, p. 12A.

13. Gerald W. Bracey, "The Assessor Assessed: A 'Revisionist' Looks at a Critique of the Sandia Report," *Journal of Educational Research*, vol. 88, no. 3 (January/February 1995): pp.141–142.

Chapter 2

1. The Virginia Declaration of Rights may be found in A. E. Dick Howard, "For the Common Benefit: The Virginia Declaration of Rights of 1776," at the end of *The George Mason Lectures: Honoring the Two Hundredth Anniversary of the Virginia Declaration of Rights*, Williamsburg, June 12, 1976, pp. 20–21. For Thomas Jefferson's original draft of the Declaration of Independence, see Julian P. Boyd, *The Declaration of Independence: The Evolution of the Text as Shown in Facsimiles of Various Drafts by Its Author, Thomas Jefferson* (Princeton, NJ.: Princeton University Press, 1945), pp. 19–21.

2. Daniel Vickers, "Competency and Competition: Economic Culture in Early America," *William and Mary Quarterly*, January 1990, p. 3.

3. Saul K. Padover, ed., *The Complete Madison: His Basic Writings* (New York: Harper and Brothers, 1973), p. 322.

4. It would have approached a contradiction in terms to say that a person had attained independence but was not competent. The property requirements of virtually all franchise laws at the time had the capability of providing the means for at least a comfortable subsistence or a minimally dignified living.

5. Vickers, "Competency and Competition," pp. 4, 7, 11, 12; Christopher L. Tomlins, *Law, Labor, and Ideology in the Early American Republic* (New York: Cambridge University Press, 1993), p. 4. A more formal definition of the idea of independence might be "the ability to attain a minimally dignified living standard, or competency, by one's own efforts through means of production under one's own ownership."

6. The word "free," in one meaning, was taken to convey a "freeholder," or "freeman," which in turn signified economic independence from another person, or the ownership and control of property sufficient to provide for a secure living for oneself. See Celeste Michelle Condit and John Louis Lucaites, *Crafting Equality: America's Anglo-African Word* (Chicago: University of Chicago Press, 1993), p. 43.

7. Ibid.

8. Jack P. Greene, *All Men Are Created Equal: Some Reflections on the Character of the American Revolution,* an inaugural lecture delivered before the University of Oxford on February 10, 1976 (Oxford: Clarendon Press, 1976), p. 18.

9. Ibid., p. 21.

10. With the passage of time, the meaning of the phrase "All men are created equal" has widened to embrace ever more categories of people, not only as the phrase itself implies but some of the founders may themselves have believed. No one today calls for a return to the narrow application of the phrase that pertained at the nation's inception.

11. Drew R. McCoy, *The Elusive Republic: Political Economy in Jeffersonian America* (New York: W. W. Norton, 1980), p. 80.

12. David Brion Davis, *Revolutions: Reflections on American Equality and Foreign Liberations* (Cambridge, Mass.: Harvard University Press, 1990), p. 20, quoting from McCoy, p. 237.

13. McCoy, *The Elusive Republic,* pp. 82–83, points out that providing a living from the land was hardly a year-round, dawn-to-dusk proposition in America at the time of the Revolution, which actually raised the problem in some people's eyes of the need to encourage and promote the work ethic beyond what a basic livelihood required. Calculations of the amount of time work required prior to the industrial revolution are found in Juliet B. Schor, *The Overworked American* (New York: Basic Books, 1991), pp. 43–48.

14. Quoted in John F. Manley, "American Liberalism and the Democratic Dream: Transcending the American Dream," *Policy Studies Review*, vol. 10, no. 1 (Fall 1990): p. 98.

15. Ibid., p. 96.

16. Ibid., p. 57.

17. Ibid., pp. 59–60.

18. Ibid., p. 100.

19. Daniel J. Boorstin, "I Am Optimistic about America," *Parade*, July 10, 1994, p. 6.

20. Manley, "American Liberalism," p. 96.

21. Vickers, "Competency and Competition," p. 18.

22. Thomas Jefferson, "First Inaugural Address," March 4, 1801, in *A Compilation of Messages and Papers of the Presidents* (New York Bureau of National Literature, 1897), vol. 1, p. 323.

23. Alexis de Tocqueville, *Democracy in America* (New York: Vintage Books, 1945), vol. 1, p. 3. As late as the 1920s, the federal government held out the promise of a homestead grant of 320 acres of land in the interior Northwest to any family willing to travel and settle there.

24. John Locke, *An Essay Concerning Human Understanding and a Treatise on the Conduct of Understanding* (Philadelphia: Hayes and Zell, 1854), p. 153 (bk. 2, chap. 21, secs. 10–11).

25. Charles Royster, *A Revolutionary People at War: The Continental Army and American Character, 1775–1783* (Chapel Hill, N.C.: University of North Carolina Press, 1979), p. 259.

26. Ibid., p. 259.

27. Ibid., p. 271.

28. Ibid., p. 268.

29. Ibid., p. 268.

30. Ibid, p. 269.

31. Ibid, p. 340.

32. Winifred Barr Rothenberg, *From Market-Places to a Market Economy: The Transformation of Rural Massachusetts, 1750–1850* (Chicago: University of Chicago Press, 1993).

33. McCoy, *The Elusive Republic*, p. 77; see also Judith N. Shklar, *American*

Citizenship: The Quest for Inclusion (Cambridge, Mass.: Harvard University Press, 1991), p. 67: "The vision of economic independence, of self-directed earning, as the ethical basis of democratic citizenship took the place of an outmoded notion of public virtue."

34. Horace Greeley, "An Address to the Printers of New York," January 17, 1850.

35. Eric Foner, *Free Soil, Free Labor, Free Men: The Ideology of the Republican Party Before the Civil War* (New York: Oxford University Press, 1970), p. 16.

36. Quoted in John E. Schwarz and Thomas J. Volgy, *The Forgotten Americans: Thirty Million Working Poor in the Land of Opportunity* (New York: W. W. Norton, 1992), p. 8.

37. A definitional element of the idea of independence is the notion that one is not dependent such as to be under the control of another's will. That is, as long as an individual is not dependent upon another, the idea of independence does not require self-sufficiency. To avert dependency for those who are not self-sufficient and who therefore produce for others, independence would require that there be a true and ready choice of employers and jobs.

One's work and effort, of course, derived from one's labor, and one owned and genuinely controlled one's own labor as long as ready options of jobs and employers existed. During the half century after the Revolution, American law increasingly protected the right of the free wage laborer, for example, to withdraw from contracts that otherwise would oblige their labor for lengthy periods of time. Particularly if there was ample alternative opportunity capable of delivering a minimally decent living, a free wage earner could give or withhold his labor as he saw fit. In this sense, at least, and to the degree it was true, the wage earner remained self-governing even in the revolutionaries' meaning of the term. The availability of a genuine choice of employments that could provide the means to a dignified living followed from the views about independence held by people like Madison and Jefferson. According to Madison: "Can any despotism be more cruel than a situation, in which the existence of thousands depends on one will, and that will on the most slight and fickle of all motives?" (quoted in Gaillard Hunt, ed., *The Writings of James Madison* [New York: G. P. Putnam's Sons, 1906], p. 100). For Jefferson's perspective, see his quote on p. 27, related to note 20.

38. McCoy, *The Elusive Republic*, p. 97.

39. Ibid., p. 124.

40. Jennifer Nedelsky, *Private Property and the Limits of American Constitutionalism: The Madisonian Framework and Its Legacy* (Chicago: University of Chicago Press, 1990), p. 43.

41. Padover, ed., *The Complete Madison*, pp. 322–23.

42. Ibid., p. 324.

43. Ibid., p. 52.

44. Nedelsky, *Private Property*, p. 45.

45. John T. Schlebecker, *Whereby We Thrive: A History of American Farming, 1607–1972* (Ames, Iowa: Iowa State University Press, 1975), p. 59.

46. Nedelsky, *Private Property*, p. 33.

47. McCoy, *The Elusive Republic*, p. 68. This same objective, for example, stood behind the belief that government ought to prohibit owners of land from the practice of primogeniture.

48. Ibid., p. 68.

49. Michael J. Sandel, *Democracy's Discontent: America in Search of a Public Philosophy* (Cambridge, Mass.: Belknap Press of Harvard University Press, 1996). See also Chapter 9, page 141, and note 12 to that chapter.

Chapter 3

1. Robert Axelrod, *The Evolution of Cooperation* (New York: Basic Books, 1984).

2. It would be difficult to measure how much of today's income distribution has been affected by the illegitimate seizure of persons and property represented by slavery, the conquest of Texas and California, and the settlement of the frontier in the United States, let alone by surely hundreds of millions of other knowing misrepresentations in dealings among Americans over the years.

3. Lying and cheating are considered so common today in our interrelationships that one teacher is reported to have advised his academic decathlon team, which performed well in a national competition: "Everybody cheats, that's just the way the world works, and we're fools just to play by the rules" (Frank Rich, "Why Is It That Every Pillar of Our Society Is Turning Out to Be a Cheat?," *Arizona Daily Star*, April 12, 1995, p. 12A).

4. Brian Barry, *Democracy, Power, and Justice* (Oxford, England: Clarendon Press, 1989), p. 487.

5. See Peter D. McClelland, *The American Search for Economic Justice* (Cambridge, Mass.: Basil Blackwell, 1990), pp. 50–87, 371–80; Friedrich A. Hayek, *The Constitution of Liberty* (Chicago: University of Chicago Press, 1960); *The Road to Serfdom* (Chicago: University of Chicago Press, 1960); and *Law, Legislation and Liberty* (Chicago: University of Chicago Press, 1976).

6. George A. Akerlof and Janet L. Yellen, *Efficiency Wage Models of the Labor Market* (Cambridge, England: Cambridge University Press, 1986); and John Dunlop, "The Task of Contemporary Wage Theory," in John Dunlop, ed., *The Theory of Wage Determination* (New York: St. Martin's Press, 1957).

7. Paul Ingrassia and Joseph B. White, *Comeback: The Fall and Rise of the American Automobile Industry* (New York: Simon and Schuster, 1994).

8. W. Edwards Demming, *Out of the Crisis* (Cambridge, Mass.: Massachusetts Institute of Technology Press, 1982), pp. ix, 6, for numerous examples of management deficiencies in the United Kingdom as they apply to failing companies, see John E. Schwarz and Thomas J. Volgy, "Experiments in Employment—A British Cure," *Harvard Business Review,* vol. 66, no. 2 (March–April, 1988): pp. 104–12.

9. Calculated from U.S. Department of Labor, *Handbook of Labor Statistics, 1989* (Washington, D.C.: Government Printing Office, 1989), p. 561, Table 146; p. 576, Table 151.

10. Richard B. Freeman, ed., *Working Under Different Rules* (New York: Russell Sage Foundation, 1994), p. 10.

11. Profits of manufacturers adjusted for inflation fell by nearly 25 percent from 1979 to 1989. Calculated from *Economic Report of the President,* 1992, p. 399, Table B-87; p. 361, Table B-56.

12. *Arizona Daily Star,* September 12, 1994, p. A5.

13. The grants received by the faculties at MIT and Harvard likely also brought employment to more people than were involved in the production of Roseanne's shows.

14. Richard Rothstein, "The Global Hiring Hall," *The American Prospect,* no. 17 (Spring 1994): p. 56.

15. Kent J. Jenkins, "For Ollie North, Crime Pays," *Washington Post National Weekly Edition,* October 18–24, 1993, p. 12.

16. Tony Horwitz, "The Six Growth Jobs Are Dull, Dead-End, Sometimes Dangerous," *Wall Street Journal*, December 1, 1994, pp. A1, A8, A9.

17. For a description of fast food employment, see Barbara Garson, *The Electronic Sweatshop: How Computers Are Transforming the Office of the Future into the Factory of the Past* (New York: Penguin, 1988), chap. 1.

18. For a powerful treatment of this subject, see Allen Buchanan, "Justice as Reciprocity Versus Subject-Centered Justice," *Philosophy and Public Affairs*, vol. 19, no. 3 (Summer 1990): pp. 227–52.

19. That attaining independence has historically been crucial to the standing of able-bodied persons in our society is frequently attested to. As political scientist Judith Shklar points out, "Citizenship in America has never been just a matter of agency and empowerment, but also of social standing as well. . . . Most Americans appear to have a clear enough idea of what [social standing] means and their relative social place, defined by income, occupation, and education, is of some importance to them" (Judith N. Shklar, *American Citizenship: The Quest for Inclusion* [Cambridge, Mass.: Harvard University Press, 1991], p. 2). Charles Murray put the point even more strongly: "A citizen in good standing was self-supporting . . . This was not only the opinion of middle-America; it was old elite wisdom as well." That is, being self-supporting has not been just another characteristic of being an American but a necessity for being considered a citizen in good standing, a necessity for basic respect and acceptance. See Charles Murray, *Losing Ground: American Social Policy, 1950–1980* (New York: Basic Books, 1984), p. 45.

20. For reasons set forth in the postscript to this chapter, this same conclusion would seem to follow if persons were acting according to rational self-interest, assuming they had no knowledge of their own ultimate status in society. Certainly it would be difficult to develop a convincing argument that rational self-interested persons not knowing their own fates would reject this conclusion in favor of some specific alternative to it. Two of the foremost alternatives that have been proposed are Robert Nozick, *Anarchy, State, and Utopia* (New York: Basic Books, 1974); and John Rawls, *A Theory of Justice* (Cambridge, Mass.: Harvard University Press, 1971).

21. The sufficient availability of opportunity presumes a genuine choice of employers. An individual cannot be said to be independent where there is no true option to make a minimally dignified living except to depend exclusively upon one employer or a trust of employers for employment. See also Chapter 2.

22. The society might well feel an obligation to assist children in the families of adults who deliberately refrain from working in an adequate job, given a choice of employments. Society could assist children in these circumstances independently through public programs attached to the schools or indirectly through programs run by philanthropic organizations.

23. Robert J. Samuelson, "End Affirmative Action," *Washington Post National Weekly Edition*, March 6–12, 1995, p. 5.

24. This conclusion, which would deny market outcomes primary status especially on matters related to independence, is entirely in keeping with the ideas of Revolutionary leaders such as Thomas Jefferson and James Madison. No one who said that government should transfer income to soften great inequalities, as did Madison, could have believed that the market should be a final arbiter. Jefferson, of course, believed that persons who were unemployed when others had a surplus had a right to occupy, farm, and reap the harvest off some of the land which produced that surplus. See Chapter 2, page 37.

25. As indicated on page 51, if the argument is true and adequate jobs are available, society owes the able-bodied poor little more than the education and training necessary to make good use of those jobs. It does not owe them welfare except possibly for transitional periods allowing them to locate new work.

26. See Chapter 2, p. 28.

27. See Chapter 1, p. 17.

28. As the postscript to this chapter suggests, the right of individuals to the opportunity to attain independence may also follow from the decision rationally self-interested individuals would make were they to enter into a social compact, assuming they had no knowledge of their own ultimate status in society. It would be difficult, in any event, to make the case that rationally self-interested persons surely would not establish this condition, in favor of some specific alternative to it, as part of a social compact.

29. This is a very different conclusion derived from the individual's rational self-interested motives than the one reached by Robert Nozick in *Anarchy, State, and Utopia* or by John Rawls in *A Theory of Justice*. I find no argument that could enable their conclusions to prevail over the ones drawn here.

Chapter 4

1. Gordon Lafer, "Measuring the Jobs Gap: Labor Demand and the Politics of Federal Employment Policy," Yale University, mimeo, August 1994, pp. 34–35.

2. Evidence indicating that many of the poor who are not employed do want to work is contained in Leonard Goodwin, *Do the Poor Want to Work?: A Social-Psychological Study of Work Orientations* (Washington, D.C.: Brookings Institution, 1972) and *Causes and Cures of Welfare: New Evidence on the Social Psychology of the Poor* (Boston: Lexington Books, 1983).

3. Daniel Vickers, "Competency and Competition: Economic Culture in Early America," *William and Mary Quarterly* (January 1990).

4. Concerning the importance of the availability of choice, see Chapter 2, note 37.

5. See Chapter 2, pages 25–26 and Chapter 9, page 141, for a statement of the reasoning behind this consideration.

6. These are important issues defining the revolutionaries' economic bottom line as to what constituted meaningful opportunity separate from the more limited criteria set forth in this study. Were they applied, far fewer employment opportunities would meet acceptable criteria than the criteria allowed in this study.

7. A widely believed maxim in America is that "through work and effort a poor person ought to be able to get someplace in this country." Suppose that Americans were asked to define this maxim. Few would deny that it means at the very least that a poor person who works hard and perseveres can move ahead and enter into the mainstream of society, at least somewhere within its lowest level. This idea of being able to reach at least the lowest level of a mainstream standard of living through hard work and perseverance has a familiar ring. It is consonant with the concept of the capacity to attain a comfortable subsistence associated in colonial times with a component of competency and thus with independence. In this way, vestiges of ideas pertaining to independence and competency still powerfully influence the mental constructs and ideals of Americans, not to mention the most abiding folklore about the country.

8. Gertrude Himmelfarb, *The Idea of Poverty: England in the Early Industrial Age* (New York: Random House, 1983), p. 61.

9. These also include a single car, an electric toaster, a television set, and frozen foods, for examples. See Dennis A. Gilbert, *Compendium of American Public Opinion* (New York: Facts on File Publications, 1988), p. 299.

10. An examination of the level of consensus about what constitutes necessities is found in Joanna Mack and Stewart Lansley, *Poor Britain* (London: George Allen and Unwin, 1985).

11. The responses of the public to the Roper survey are presented in *The Public Perspective*, vol. 6, no. 1 (November/December 1994): p. 98; for the results of the Gallup surveys going back to 1947, see *Gallup Report*, no. 248 (May 1986): p. 3.

12. I have projected the federal poverty line from 1963 back to 1950, using the consumer price index. The public response to the Gallup question came to 113 percent of the poverty line in 1954 and about 102 percent in 1950.

13. *Statistical Abstract of the United States, 1956*, p. 515, Table 6; p. 553, Table 674; p. 782, Table 983. See also *American Almanac, 1973* (New York: Grosset and Dunlap), p. 691, Table 1162.

14. While the poverty line was first calculated for 1963, the most recent consumption data upon which it was based were for 1955.

15. The average American household owns between two and three automobiles.

16. This budget is an updated version of the economy budget for 1990 found in John E. Schwarz and Thomas J. Volgy, *The Forgotten Americans: Thirty Million Working Poor in the Land of Opportunity* (New York: W. W. Norton, 1992), pp. 42–46. A more detailed account of the budget can be found there. Two items have been added to the budget: $400 has been added for public transportation and $400 to pay job-related expenses for two workers.

17. Questions have been raised about local variations in the cost of living across the nation and whether such local variations should be taken into consideration in developing a measure of income adequacy. ACCRA (formerly the American Chamber of Commerce Researchers' Association) reports a price index for numerous metropolitan areas across the nation based on a budget for what it describes as a mid-management family. Across locales, the relative cost patterns of this budget and lower family budgets compiled by the Bureau of Labor Statistics are similar. How much difference is there in the cost of living across different communities? In fewer than 7 percent of the cities and towns ACCRA measured did the cost of living fall below 90 percent of the average cost. Many of them were comparatively small places such as Dothan, Alabama, Joplin, Missouri, and Pueblo, Colorado. In virtually none of the locales did the cost of living fall below 85 percent of the average. The variation by greater than 15 percent was *above* the average cost of living, sometimes considerably above, as in New York City (213 percent). In these instances of very substantial variance from the average—all of them varia- tions above the average cost—it is probably true to say that the family bud- get detailed on pages 63–64 is flawed. If so, use of the family budget as a standard of income adequacy across the nation would likely understate rather than overstate problems of economic opportunity. For more than one hun- dred selected ACCRA results, see the *Statistical Abstract of the United States, 1992*, pp. 474–75, Table 745; and *1993*, pp. 487–88, Table 763.

18. Schwarz and Volgy, *The Forgotten Americans*, pp. 38–39, Christopher Jencks and Kathryn Edin, "The Real Welfare Problem," *The American Prospect*, no. 1 (Spring 1990): pp. 32–35.

19. Schwarz and Volgy, *The Forgotten Americans*, p. 41, Table 3. The reference is to families with incomes up to 150 percent of the poverty line, which would be about $23,000 for a family of four in 1994.

20. Vickers, "Competency and Competition."

21. Research on four hundred day care centers in California, Colorado, Con- necticut, and North Carolina shows that parents have a right to be concerned about leaving their children in day care, considering the highly uneven and often poor quality of the care. (See Susan Chira, "Care at Most Child Day Centers Rated as Poor," *New York Times*, February 7, 1955, p. A12). Low- cost day care centers can be overcrowded, ill-run, and understaffed. They can also be unhygienic. Whatever the quality of the center, in fact, children under age two in day care are from four to thirty-six times more likely (depending on the size of the day care center) than children who remain at home to catch pneumococcal infections, which are the leading cause of earaches, pneumo- nia, and meningitis ("Infection Risk Worse in Big Day-Care Center, Study Finds," *Arizona Daily Star*, March 15, 1955, p. A2, from findings published in the *Journal of the American Medical Association*). Working families unable to spend much on day care thus often face a Hobson's choice.

22. If the second earner in a low-wage household worked full-time instead of three-quarters time and from this received, say, an additional $3,250 more in pay a year (from a wage of $6.50 per hour for five hundred hours), federal and state taxes and Social Security would take about $800. Moderately low-cost care for two children for two and a half hours each during the afternoons would add approximately $2,200 more over the school year and the summer. These two expenses alone total practically the whole of the $3,300 increase in pay brought in by the extra five hundred hours of work.

23. Rebecca Blank has demonstrated that part-time jobs pay hourly wages of about 80 percent of full-time jobs for the same occupational category and level of education and skill. She suggests that part of the reason may be the lower productivity of part-time workers because such workers "are often focused on their activities outside the job." In addition, part-time jobs may pay lower wages because they are inherently less productive jobs. In any case, part-time workers, on average, earn an hourly wage that is about 20 percent beneath that for full-time work for the same occupational category and level of education and skill. See Rebecca M. Blank, "Are Part-Time Jobs Bad Jobs?," in Gary Burtless, ed., *A Future of Lousy Jobs?: The Changing Structure of U.S. Wages* (Washington, D.C.: Brookings Institution, 1990), pp. 123–65, esp. 132, 153.

24. This is to say that the prime earner would be earning 60.6 percent of the total earnings. For 1994, 60.6 percent of $25,000 is $15,150, requiring a wage of $7.58 per hour over two thousand hours of work.

25. An adequate job need not offer as many as two thousand hours. Fewer hours than two thousand would suffice, down to fifteen hundred hours, as long as the total earnings requirement is met. Jobs falling below fifteen hundred hours are not considered adequate since they frequently do not offer benefits. Steady year-round full-time jobs, rather than the piecing together of two or three part-time jobs, are taken as a base-line both because part-time jobs normally do not offer benefits and because it can be difficult to assure that the schedules of two or more part-time jobs remain aligned over considerable periods of time. Part-time jobs are particularly vulnerable to schedule changes and irregular hours.

26. Calculations of the amount of time that work required prior to the industrial revolution are found in Juliet B. Schor, *The Overworked American* (New York: Basic Books, 1991), pp. 43–48.

27. An adequate income for a single parent with one child in 1994 was $16,600. Including the average court-awarded low-income absent-parent payment for one child of about $2,000, that left $14,600 to be earned by the single parent (requiring an hourly wage of $7.30 over two thousand hours of work). Note, however, that the $16,600 budget has no provision for child care which most full-time single working parents would require. An adequate income for a single parent with two children in 1994 was $19,500. With $4,000 in absent-parent payments for two children, the single parent would need to earn $15,500, requiring an hourly wage of $7.75. For the size of absent-parent payments awarded by courts, including low-income absent parents, see the *Statistical Abstract of the United States, 1993*, p. 385, Table 612. It is of note that courts awarded *no* child-support payments to 4.2 million single parents, including 1.8 million whose incomes were beneath the poverty line. See ibid., Table 611.

28. The budget for a single person would allow $2,180 for food; $3,420 for housing ($200 per month for rent and $85 per month for all utilities and phone); $3,300 for the operation of a single car; $1,200 for health insurance co-payments and medical expenses; $300 for clothes and shoes; $2,000 for personal expenses (such as toothpaste, household cleaning products, towels, postage stamps, and so forth) and for the repair or replacement of household items (dishes, bedding, and furniture, for examples); and $2,460 for federal and state taxes and social security. This budget for one person is a version of the economy budget presented in John E. Schwarz and Thomas J. Volgy, *The Forgotten Americans* (New York: W. W. Norton, 1992), pp. 42–46.

29. The most obvious possible exception to this generalization concerns a small minority of households. This is the married-couple household with two potential incomes but with no children and in which there never have been any children (couples that once had children rarely voluntarily move down to lower-paying jobs when the children leave the household). The number of ever-married women who have never had any children (including adopted children) by forty years of age and who were married in 1994 and not of retirement age can be estimated at around 3 million. (Estimated from data provided in *Statistical Abstract of the United States, 1993*, p. 80, Table 106; p. 54, Table 61). Undoubtedly, considerably fewer of these women knew, when they were younger, that they would never want to have children. Similarly, married couples with only one child often do not know for certain that they will never want another child (most ultimately do have another child), and certainly would not want this deeply personal decision to result from the inadequacies of their employment and inability to get a job capable of supporting a second child decently.

30. For the hours devoted to house-related activities, see Schor, *The Overworked American*, p. 35, Table 2.3.

31. Appendix A describes the methodology used to make determinations about the number of never-filled vacancies and untapped opportunities for self-employment. The two categories together for 1989 (the last conclusion of a business cycle) amounted to 2.9 million adequate job opportunities above and beyond the employment otherwise available during that year—a figure greater than the *total* job creation for the year, which came to 2.7 million net new jobs, including part-time and low-wage full-time jobs.

32. I define households dependent upon employment as also including all secondary individuals (whom the Census does not categorize as householders) if they occupy year-round full-time jobs with adequate wages. Such persons are not included unless they occupy adequate jobs. They are then accounted for by subtracting the adequate jobs they hold from the total supply of adequate jobs.

33. Bryce Christensen et al, *The Family Wage: Work, Gender, and Children in the Modern Economy* (Rockford, Ill.: Rockford Institute, 1988), p. 19.

Chapter 5

1. Unless otherwise noted, the analysis of data in this chapter is based on the Panel Survey of Income Dynamics (PSID) adjusted to the population and employment estimates of the Bureau of the Census's Current Population Survey (CPS).

2. Gary S. Becker, "Family Economics and Macro Behavior," *American Economic Review*, vol. 78, no. 1 (March 1988): p. 11.

3. The total number of households with heads under age sixty-five came to 73.2 million in 1989. Excluding households with heads under age sixty-five that did not occupy adequate jobs because they were either seriously disabled or early retired reduced the number of households to 66.5 million. Heads of households reporting that they were somewhat disabled are included in the totals for households. While serious disablement is a severe impediment to attaining an adequate job, the same does not hold for persons reporting that they are somewhat disabled. Their rates of employment in adequate jobs are broadly similar to those of the remainder of the population. Figures and con-

clusions about households and adequate jobs reported here and elsewhere, unless noted otherwise, are calculated based on the Panel Survey of Income Dynamics (PSID) checked against the Current Population Survey (CPS) for population estimates.

4. Recall that an adequate job is a year-round full-time job that pays a base-line wage ($6.10 an hour or better in 1989) for two thousand hours of work, or pays a wage resulting in equivalent earnings (about $12,200) for no less than fifteen hundred hours over the year (this represents thirty hours a week, the usual threshold for benefits). Thus, adequate jobs include employment less than year-round full-time, to thirty hours a week, as long as the total earnings from such jobs are adequate. Similarly, jobs requiring more than two thousand hours a year but paying the base-line hourly wage or higher, which often is the situation, for example, during the early years in many professions, are counted as adequate jobs.

Excluding adequate jobs occupied by workers over age sixty-four, workers who were seriously disabled, and unrelated individuals not counted as householders or secondary members of a household (these three groups took 4.6 million adequate jobs in total), the number of adequate jobs available to households with heads under age sixty-five came to 61.7 million in 1989. This total of 61.7 million adequate jobs includes 500,000 untaken adequate jobs that were available but never filled and, in addition, 2.4 million adequate jobs that might have been created through self-employment if we presume that a doubling of successful self-employment activity had been possible (see Appendix A). The total number of households needing to be accommodated by these adequate jobs came to 66.5 million (see note 3, above). The resulting shortfall in jobs amounted to 4.8 million. Supplemental earners from households already occupying an adequate job took up 10.9 million such jobs, thus leaving a shortage of 15.7 million adequate jobs as compared to the number of households dependent upon employment for a living.

With respect to these calculations, jobs paying base-line earnings or greater—$12,200 or more in 1989—only by requiring more than two thousand hours of work over a year (all such jobs thus paid less than a base-line wage) were not counted as adequate jobs. There were 860,000 jobs in 1989 where workers reached the base-line earnings level only by working up to twenty-five hundred hours. An additional 1.3 million jobs required workers to be on the job up to three thousand hours (sixty hours a week) in order to reach the base-line earnings level. A final 1.7 million jobs paid the base-line earnings only if their occupants worked in excess of three thousand hours during the year.

Adequate jobs, of course, are not synonymous with the notion of year-round full-time jobs. There was a total of 80.2 million year-round full-time workers in 1989, according to the U.S. Bureau of the Census (see *Current Population Reports*, Series P-60, no. 178, p. 25, Table 4). Including those occupied by disabled persons and persons over age sixty-four, and including adjustments for never-filled jobs and self-employment, adequate jobs totaled 66.3 million in 1989.

5. Each of these households occupied two or more adequate jobs.

6. In 1989 supplemental earners took 10.9 million adequate jobs. Had the excluded households gotten half (5.5 million) of these jobs, about 10.2 million households would have been without such a job, instead of 15.7 million.

7. For a discussion of the natural rate of unemployment and the logic behind it, see Paul Krugman, *Peddling Prosperity: Economic Sense and Nonsense in the Age of Diminished Expectations* (New York: W. W. Norton, 1994), pp. 40–47.

8. A high school diploma was the modal education, held by a plurality of workers. Slightly greater than half of the entering labor force in 1989 had attained that level of education or less. *Statistical Abstract of the United States, 1993*, p. 153, Table 232. For adults aged twenty-five to thirty-four, 51.2 percent had no education beyond high school. Regarding the undereducated, the view requiring the completion of a high school degree would conflict with the legitimate interests of individuals whose natural capacities do not enable them to finish that level of education. Other provisions for assistance would need to be made available to them.

9. Workers above age sixty entered the labor force at a time when it was still highly common to have completed less than a high school degree. Thus, the analysis presented in the remainder of the paragraph excludes all households headed by persons without a high school degree through age sixty.

10. Among workers aged sixteen to sixty-five.

11. Based on the achievement motivation instrument contained in the Panel Survey of Income Dynamics.

12. Rick Bragg, "Big Holes Where the Dignity Used to Be," *New York Times*, March 5, 1996, p. A10.

13. Discouraged workers who had left the labor force are included in the unemployment figure. All household heads, without regard to the number of children in the household, fared slightly better. Of those employed year-round full-time below an adequate wage in 1979, 43 percent were still employed below an adequate wage in 1989 and 8.1 percent were unemployed.

14. For male household heads with two or more children and some education beyond high school (but not a college diploma), for example, 62 percent who worked year-round full-time for less than an adequate wage in 1979 either were still earning less than an adequate wage in 1989 (57 percent) or were unemployed (5 percent).

15. Louis Uchitelle, "The Humbling of the Harvard Man," *New York Times*, March 6, 1994, pp. F1, F8.

16. Of households heads with a high school degree or some education beyond high school (but not a college diploma) who were earning less than an adequate wage in 1979, 64 percent ended the period earning less than an adequate wage even if they worked year-round full-time the entire decade.

17. Leslie Phillips, "A Family's Tale," *USA Today*, January 3, 1995, p. 6A.

18. Jeff Rowe, "Fast Food Industry Features a Fast Track," *Arizona Daily Star*, March 7, 1994, p. 8D.

19. Gail Buchalter, "What Failure Taught Me," *Parade*, January 15, 1995, p. 4.

20. The illustrations that follow are from personal interviews taken from 1990 to 1994. Names have been changed and incomes put into 1995 dollars.

21. George J. Borjas, *Friends and Strangers: The Impact of Immigrants in the U.S. Economy* (New York: Basic Books, 1990), p. 231, Table A2. Median school years completed for American males in 1980 was 15.7 years, and the 1975–80 wave of immigrants from Japan, it was 15.7 years, Korea 14.0 years, and Vietnam 12.8 years. The educational level was similar for each of these nationalities of immigrants taken as a group, regardless of year of entry.

22. The poverty rate in 1980 for the immigrant population from Japan was 13.0 percent, Korea 13.5 percent, Vietnam 37.0 percent, and all immigrants 15.2 percent. For the native-born it was 11.7 percent (Borjas, *Friends and Strangers*, p. 147, Table 8.4; p. 236, Table A7).

23. Borjas, *Friends and Strangers*, pp. 154–55, Table 9.2, on welfare recipiency, shows that both male- and female-headed households immigrating to the United States between 1950 and 1959 had higher rates of welfare recipiency than the native population thirty years later.

24. In order to examine hourly wages and changes in hourly wages over time for individuals, data must include information about total earnings and total number of hours worked for each individual and must apply to the same individuals for the time period under examination. The current population surveys do not interview the same individuals and heads of households consistently over a lengthy time period. Prior to 1973 they also contain information about hours employed in categories too broad to determine hourly earnings over a year, especially for supervisory and nonproduction workers and for workers on the job for more than 1,750 hours in a year. A database that contains the appropriate data both to determine hourly earnings for all employed workers and to do so for the same individuals over a lengthy time span is the Panel Survey of Income Dynamics (PSID), which serves as the foundation for this study. The earliest year for which PSID data are available is 1967.

25. Alan B. Wilson, Travis Hirschi, and Glen Elder, "Richmond Youth Project: Secondary School Study, Technical Report #1," (Survey Research Center, University of California, Berkeley, mimeo, 1965, p. 4/28–31, response to question 4/28.

26. Ibid, p. 4/66–70, response to question 4/68.

27. Ibid., p. 2/61–64, response (disagree or strongly disagree) to question 2/64.

28. Hourly wage data are not generally available on an annual basis prior to the first year of the Panel Survey on Income Dynamics, in 1967. See note 24.

29. *The American Almanac for 1973* (New York: Grosset and Dunlap), p. 219, Table 346.

30. David Frum, *Dead Right* (New York: Basic Books, 1994), p. 100.

31. See Chapters 6 and 8.

32. For growth rates of the British economy during the nineteenth century, see Peter Mathias, *The First Industrial Nation: An Economic History of Britain, 1700–1914*, 2d ed. (London: Routledge, 1983), p. 222, Table IVd. Real growth rates of the British economy over multiyear periods from 1801 to 1901 varied from 2.2 percent to 3.3 percent yearly, averaging about 2.7 percent, enough for the economy to multiply by more than seven times over the century. During the twenty-year period from 1973 to 1993 the American economy's growth averaged just over 2.3 percent a year. From 1979 to 1989, the economy grew by 2.2 percent a year.

33. A total of 7.6 million net new adequate jobs were added from 1979 to

1989. Net increases of persons over age sixty-four and unrelated nonhouse-holders occupying these jobs account for 1.9 million of them, which left a net increase of 5.7 million new adequate jobs for households headed by persons under age sixty-five.

34. Data for Germany, France, Great Britain, and Italy are in *Statistical Abstract of the United States, 1993*, p. 859, Table 1403.

35. Unrelated individuals referred to are persons such as guests or lodgers whom the Census does not count as householders.

36. The birth rate giving rise to the baby boom generation (the generation born from 1947 through 1964) was one third higher than the birth rate of the 1930s and greater still in comparison with that of the early 1940s. When the generation born in the 1930s and early 1940s turned adult in the 1950s, about 7.4 million new nonelderly households came into being from 1950 to 1960. A rise by one third in this number to reflect the higher birth rate of the 1950s and early 1960s suggests that the baby boomer generation should have experienced a growth of 9.8 million new nonelderly households over the period of a decade, or 2.4 million greater than from 1950 to 1960. The actu-al growth in demand from such households from 1979 to 1989 was 0.5 mil-lion more than that, or 10.3 million. The growth figures for 1979 to 1989 are for nonelderly able-bodied householders.

37. To date, evidence has been gathered in the United States and elsewhere concerning the overall number of jobs and not the number of adequate jobs. With respect to the overall number of jobs, no industrial nation has seen an increase that comes close proportionately to the one represented by the Unit-ed States from 1967 to 1979 in new adequate jobs—about 1.2 million a year over those years. It involves a rise of more than 2 percent a year, each and every year on average. Overall job growth in the European economies has typically been below 1 percent and in the Japanese economy about 1 percent. None has been able to average 2 percent a year or more over a decade-long period or longer.

38. Based on the percentage annual increase in the economy since 1973, the creation of 2.6 million jobs per year on average is a reasonable expectation.

39. The coming retirement of the baby-boom generation, expected to begin in full force around 2010, may result in a decline in the net growth of demand for adequate jobs thereafter. Even taking this expected decline into account, however, along with the expected increase of young workers from the shadow baby-boomer bulge, it will require that more than a generation—fully twenty-four years—of continuously strong job growth every year without any slowdown or recession for the nation to be able to bridge the present job deficit.

Chapter 6

1. Calculated from *Economic Report of the President,* 1992, p. 346, Table B-42; and Council of Economic Advisors, *Economic Indicators,* February 1995.

2. Unless otherwise noted, the analysis of the chapter is based on annual survey data from the Panel Survey on Income Dynamics adjusted to the population estimates of the Current Population Survey.

3. Employed one thousand hours or more in each year.

4. For poll results in the 1990s (and comparisons with the 1980s), see Clay Chandler, "Is It Half Empty, or Half Full?," *Washington Post National Weekly Edition,* July 29–August 4, 1996, p. 18; and Rick Bragg, "Big Holes Where the Dignity Used to Be," *New York Times,* March 5, 1996, p. A9.

5. See Chapter 5, p. 88.

6. On governmental spending, taxation, and regulation, see Chapter 8. On the effect of global competition, see pp. 93–94.

7. Gary Burtless, "Earnings Inequalities over the Business Cycles," in Gary Burtless, ed., *A Future of Lousy Jobs?: The Changing Structure of U.S. Wages* (Washington, D.C.: Brookings Institution, 1990), p. 116, Table A-1. See also note 8.

8. In making this estimate, I have eliminated half of the difference in inequality among males shown by Burtless (see note 7) as caused by factors other than earnings. See Lynn A. Karoly and Gary Burtless, "Demographic Changes, Rising Earnings Inequality, and the Distribution of Personal Well-being," *Demography,* vol. 32, no. 3 (August 1995): pp. 379–406. The authors find that unequal wages account for 40 percent of the increased earnings disparity directly and an unspecified amount indirectly through the effect of lower wages on reduced work.

9. Calculated from figures provided by the Bureau of Labor Statistics using the government's new chain method of calculation.

10. Here it is appropriate to use wage figures applying to different mixes of workers in two different years, instead of the same workers in those two years, because the productivity figures are also based on the output of the different mix of workers. It is also appropriate here to use average pay since the comparison is to average productivity. For the increase in real compensation, see *Economic Report of the President*, 1992, p. 348, Table B-44; *Economic Indicators*, March 1995, p. 16.

11. Adjusting compensation over time for inflation is typically carried out by using the consumer price index to measure inflation. There has been some criticism of the CPI. Using a different measure of inflation (the personal consumption implicit inflator, or PEC deflator), Matthew D. Shapiro found that PCE-deflated compensation per hour grew at 0.6 percent annually instead of less than 0.4 percent from 1972 to 1992, or a total of about 15 percent over those years (p. 337). During the same years, overall productivity of workers, using the government's chain method of calculation, grew at 32 percent, a 17 percent difference with compensation over those twenty years. For the compensation figures, see Matthew D. Shapiro, "Comments and Discussion," *Brookings Papers on Economic Activity*, vol. 1 (1994): p. 337. See also Barry Bosworth and George L. Perry, "Productivity and Real Wages: Is There a Puzzle?," *Brookings Papers on Economic Activity*, vol. 1 (1994): pp. 317–44. This 17 percent difference between productivity and real compensation comes to about 0.7 percent per year.

12. Paul Krugman, *Peddling Prosperity: Economic Sense and Nonsense in the Age of Diminished Expectations* (New York: W. W. Norton, 1994), pp. 146–48.

13. See John E. Schwarz and Thomas J. Volgy, *The Forgotten Americans: Thirty Million Working Poor in the Land of Opportunity* (New York: W. W. Norton, 1992), pp. 86–88, for the figures and sources relating to conclusions reached in this and the next sentences.

14. Sheldon Danziger and Peter Gottschalk, *America Unequal* (Cambridge, Mass.: Harvard University Press, 1995), pp. 139–40.

15. Thomas J. Volgy, John E. Schwarz, and Lawrence E. Imwalle, "In Search of Economic Well-being: The Relation Between Worker Power and Economic Returns in Ten Industrial Nations," *American Journal of Political Science*, vol. 40, no. 4 (November 1996): pp. 1233–1252.

16. Calculated from *Statistical Abstract of the United States*, 1965, p. 217, Table 297; and 1993, p. 401, Table 635.

17. *Statistical Abstract of the United States, 1993*, p. 152, Table 230.

18. Edward F. Denison, *Why Growth Rates Differ: Postwar Experience in Nine Western Countries* (Washington, D.C.: Brookings Institution, 1967), documents the importance of educational advancement to productivity improvement in the United States prior to 1970.

19. See the postscript to Chapter 5, and also page 91 and note 4 of this chapter, on trends from 1989 through 1995.

Chapter 7

1. See chapters 1 through 3.

2. Jennifer L. Hochschild, "The Double-Edged Sword of Equal Opportunity," in Ian Shapiro and Grant Reeher, eds., *Power, Inequality, and Democratic Politics: Essays in Honor of Robert A. Dahl* (Boulder, Colo.: Westview Press, 1988), p. 184 (pp. 168–200).

3. Christopher Jencks et al., *Inequality: A Reassessment of the Effect of Family and Schooling in America* (New York: Basic Books, 1972), found the income disparity between whites and blacks in 1961 to be about 25 to 35 percent for comparably educated and skilled workers. Finis Welch, "Black-White Differences in Returns to Schooling," *American Economic Review*, vol. 63 (December 1973): p. 897, shows that after 1958 this gap was narrower for newly entering workers, holding each extra year of education constant, by 4 to 8 percent, because by the late 1950s and early 1960s additional education had a 4 percent greater payoff to newly entering blacks when compared with their base than was the case for whites; the figure had grown to 8 percent by the mid-1960s. Young black males of comparable education and aptitude to whites, through a high school degree, continued to receive lower wages well beyond the 1960s. See John E. Schwarz and Thomas J. Volgy, *The Forgotten Americans: Thirty Million Working Poor in the Land of Opportunity* (New York: W. W. Norton, 1992), pp. 78–80; Richard B. Freeman and Harry J. Holzer, eds., *The Black Youth Employment Crisis* (Chicago: University of Chicago Press, 1986), for the early 1980s; and Katherine Newman and Chauncy Lennon, "The Job Ghetto," *The American Prospect*, no. 122 (Summer 1995): pp. 66–67.

4. *Economic Report of the President*, 1992, p. 338, Table B-35. The rates among black males fell from 61.5 percent in 1956 to 47.4 percent in 1970, while the rates among whites declined from 60.4 to 57.5 percent. Less than half of the decline in either group during this period can be attributed to increasing rates of enrollment in school. From 1956 to 1963 the rate among black males fell from 61.5 percent to 51.5 percent; the rate among whites declined from 60.4 percent to 53.1 percent. A recent study of teenagers has shown that between 20 and 40 percent of the differences in the employment rates of central-city teenagers by race is explained by the distance jobs are located from the teens' residences. See Keith R. Ihlanfeldt, *Job Accessibility and the Employment and School Enrollment of Teenagers* (Kalamazoo, Mich.: W. E. Upjohn Institute for Employment Research, 1992). For the conditions prevailing in the late 1960s and their effects on labor force participation, see Carolyn S. Bell, *The Economics of the Ghetto* (New York: Pegasus, 1970), esp. pp. 107–17.

5. Quoted in Gertrude Himmelfarb, *The Idea of Poverty: England in the Early Industrial Age* (New York: Vintage, 1983), p. 52.

6. Ibid., p. 52.

7. Bayard Rustin and Tom Kahn, "Civil Rights," *Commentary*, vol. 39, no. 6 (June 1965): p. 45.

8. Bradley R. Schiller, *The Economics of Poverty and Discrimination* (Englewood Cliffs, N.J.: Prentice-Hall, 1980), p. 54.

9. Gordon Lafer, "Minority Unemployment: Labor Market Segmentation and the Failure of Job-Training Policy in New York City," *Urban Affairs Quarterly*, vol. 28, no. 2 (December 1992): pp. 210–13.

10. Newman and Lennon, "The Job Ghetto," p. 66.

11. Congressional Budget Office, "In Pursuit of Higher Wages and Employment-Based Health Insurance," February 1993, p. 10, Table 1. Only college graduates had a statistically significant percentage increase in wages, and only their wage increases exceeded the 4 percent rate of inflation during the period.

12. See Chapter 5, pages 76–77.

13. Recall that the federal poverty line itself, established under the auspices of the War on Poverty, had been created as a measure of the lowest level of the prevailing or mainstream standard of living and was moored to the spending patterns of families within the mainstream. See the discussion in Chapter 4 and in Schwarz and Volgy, *The Forgotten Americans*, pp. 32–36, for a summary of the development of the poverty line.

14. Jonathan Alter, "The Brain and the Pig Trough," *Newsweek*, February 15, 1993, p. 27.

15. Nancy Gibbs, "The Vicious Cycle," *Time*, June 20, 1994, p. 33.

16. Elizabeth Shogren, "Discord Among GOP Senators Threatens to Stall Welfare Bill," *Los Angeles Times*, June 16, 1995, p. A4.

17. Gibbs, "The Vicious Cycle," p. 26, reporting the results of a Time/CNN poll. See also Richard Morin, "The Devil Is in the Details," *Washington Post National Weekly Edition*, January 30–February 5, 1995, p. 37, citing results from a Kaiser/Harvard Survey.

18. Morin, "The Devil Is in the Details," p. 37.

19. This view, strictly speaking, is in error. At its inception, the welfare system was intended to aid widows with children. It was understood that their households might need assistance for longer than temporary periods, until the children turned adult.

20. Robert Haveman, "From Welfare to Work: Problems and Pitfalls, *Focus*, vol. 18, no. 1 (special issue, 1996): p. 22.

21. Quoted in Jon Nordheimer, "Welfare-to-Work Plans Show Success Is Difficult to Achieve," *New York Times*, September 1, 1996, p. 10.

22. In-depth interviews with welfare mothers by Christopher Jencks and Kathryn Edin, "The Real Welfare Problem," *The American Prospect*, no. 1 (Spring 1990): pp. 31–50, found that 60 percent of the welfare mothers surveyed worked part-time at off-the-books jobs or held regular jobs under assumed names. See also Joel F. Handler, *The Poverty of Welfare Reform* (New Haven, Conn.: Yale University Press, 1995), pp. 52–53.

23. Jason De Parle, "When Giving Up Welfare for a Job Just Doesn't Pay," *New York Times*, July 8, 1992, pp. A1, A15.

24. Some organizations, such as America Works, are able, using an elaborate network of personal connections, to locate better jobs for welfare recipients, but even they work with a relative handful of recipients at a time and also shy away from recipients least capable of doing well in the labor market.

25. Fifty-three percent of public assistance recipients rank in the lowest fifth of the population in mental aptitude. See Gordon Berlin and Andrew Sum, *Toward a More Perfect Union: Basic Skills, Poor Families and Our Economic Future* (New York: Ford Foundation, 1988), occasional paper no. 3, p. 29, Table 7, based on the Armed Forces Qualification Test.

26. David Whitman, "The Myth of Reform," *U.S. News & World Report*, January 16, 1995, p. 32.

27. Gibbs, "The Vicious Cycle," p. 28.

28. Barbara Vobejda, "Training for Work from Welfare," *Washington Post National Weekly Edition*, July 7–13, 1995, p. 30. For a comprehensive review of the effects of workfare experimental programs, see Daniel Friedlander and Gary Burtless, *Five Years After: The Long-term Effects of Welfare-to-Work Programs* (New York: Russell Sage Foundation, 1995).

29. Morin, "The Devil Is in the Details," p. 37.

30. Douglas J. Besharov, "Not All Single Mothers Are Created Equal," *The American Enterprise*, vol. 3, no. 5 (September/October 1992): pp. 16–17.

31. Surveys of the Kerner Commission in 1967 and the Richmond Youth Project (Contra Costa, Calif.) in 1964 indicate that large numbers of young persons believed that opportunity was inadequate. For results of the Kerner Commission survey, see *Report of the National Advisory Commission on Civil Disorders* (New York: Bantam Books, 1968), pp. 132–33, 175; for the results of the Richmond Youth Project, see Chapter 5, pages 81–82.

32. Quoted in Ann Hulbert, "Single Parent Families: Children as Parents," *Current*, December 1984, pp. 8–9.

33. Bayard Rustin, "From Protest to Politics: The Civil Rights Movement," *Commentary*, vol. 39, no. 2 (February 1965): p. 27.

34. Ibid., pp. 26–27; Rustin and Kahn, "Civil Rights," p. 45.

35. The incidence of teen illegitimacy rose by 14 percent from 1945 to 1950; 23 percent from 1950 to 1955; and 26 percent from 1955 to 1960. It then rose by 41 percent from 1960 to 1965 and 54 percent from 1965 to 1970. As a percentage of all births to all women regardless of age, illegitimate births accounted for 4.1 percent in 1945, 3.9 percent in 1950, 4.5 percent in 1955, 5.3 percent in 1960, 7.7 percent in 1965, and 10.8 percent in 1970, leading to a proportionate rise from 1950 to 1955 of 15 percent; 18 percent from 1955 to 1960, 45 percent from 1960 to 1965; and 40 percent from 1965 to 1970.

36. Mike Males, "Poverty, Rape, Adult/Teen Sex: Why Pregnancy Prevention Programs Don't Work," *Phi Delta Kappan*, January 1994, p. 409, found a correlation of 0.81 for teenage births in the fifty states and the youth poverty rates of those states. That is, the incidence of youth poverty by itself explains nearly two thirds of the variance in the incidence of teenage births in the states. See also D. P. Hogan and E. M. Kitagawa, "The Impact of Social Status, Family Structure, and Neighborhood on the Fertility of Black

Adolescents," *American Journal of Sociology*, vol. 90, no. 4 (1985): p. 852.

37. The lowest quarter of the income scale ends approximately at the level of a base-line income. In 1990, for example, about 24 percent of the population lived in households that had less than a base-line income.

38. Elijah Anderson, "Sex Codes and Family Life Among Poor Inner-City Youths," *Annals of the American Academy of Political and Social Science*, vol. 501 (January 1989): p. 76.

39. Douglas J. Besharov, "Born to Lose: Welfare Reform Will Work Only If It Addresses the Problem of Out-of-Wedlock Births," *Washington Post National Weekly Edition*, December 20–26, 1993, p. 24.

40. Naomi B. Farber, "The Significance of Aspirations Among Unmarried Adolescent Mothers," *Social Service Review*, December 1989, pp. 518–32.

41. Elaine McCrate, "Labor Market Segmentation and Relative Black/White Teenage Birth Rates," *Review of Black Political Economy*, vol. 18 (Spring 1990): pp. 37–53; D. M. Upchurch and J. McCarthy, "The Timing of a First Birth and High School Completion," *American Sociological Review*, vol. 55 (1990): pp. 224–34.

42. Randall J. Olsen and George Farkas, "The Effect of Economic Opportunity and Family Background on Adolescent Cohabitation and Childbearing Among Low-Income Blacks, *Journal of Labor Economics*, vol. 8, no. 3 (1990): pp. 341–62, especially the findings relating to what Olsen and Farkas call "the opportunity-cost argument" (p. 342).

43. See Ibid.; J. C. Cramer, "Employment Trends of Young Mothers and the Opportunity Costs of Babies in the United States," *Demography*, vol. 16 (1979): pp. 177–97; E. Jones, "Ways in Which Childbearing Affects Women's Employment: Evidence from the National Fertility Study," *Population Studies*, vol. 36, no. 1 (1982): pp. 5–14; Greg J. Duncan and Saul D. Hoffman, "Welfare Benefits, Economic Opportunities, and Out-of-Wedlock Births Among Teenage Girls," *Demography*, vol. 27, no. 4 (November 1990): pp. 519–35; R. D. Plotnick and S. Lundberg, "Adolescent Premarital Childbearing," discussion paper no. 926–90, Institute for Research on Poverty, Madison, Wis.; and, P. A. Jargowsky, "Ghetto Poverty Among Blacks in the 1980s," *Journal of Policy Analysis and Management*, vol. 13, no. 2 (1994): pp. 288–310.

44. Besharov, "Born to Lose," p. 24.

45. Arline T. Geronimus and Sanders Korenman, "The Socioeconomic Consequences of Teen Childbearing Reconsidered," *Quarterly Journal of Economics*, vol. 107, no. 4 (November 1992): pp. 1187–1214; Arline T. Geronimus, "Teenage Childbearing and Social and Reproductive Disadvantage: The Evolution of Complex Questions and the Demise of Simple Answers," *Family Relations*, vol. 40 (October 1991): pp. 463–71. See also Upchurch and McCarthy, "The Timing of a First Birth and High School Completion," who report from their sample that most females who got pregnant had *already* dropped out of high school and that most who got pregnant while still in high school did go on to graduate.

46. Kristin Luker, "Dubious Conceptions: The Controversy over Teen Pregnancy," *The American Prospect*, vol. 5 (Spring 1991): pp. 73–83, esp. pp. 77–78.

47. Frank Furstenberg, Jr., "As the Pendulum Swings: Teenage Childbearing and Social Concern," *Family Relations*, vol. 40, no. 2 (April 1991): p. 136.

48. Figures on the spread of premarital sex are found in Douglas J. Besharov with Karen N. Gardiner in "Truth and Consequences: Teen Sex," *The American Enterprise*, January–February 1993, pp. 54–56.

49. Besharov and Gardiner, "Truth and Consequences," p. 57. See also Hogan and Kitawaga, "The Impact of Social Status" and Sandra L. Hanson, David E. Meyers, and Alan L. Ginsburg, "The Role of Responsibility and Knowledge in Reducing Teenage Out-of-Wedlock Childbearing," *Journal of Marriage and Family*, vol. 49, no. 2 (May 1987): p. 250.

50. Welfare recipiency turned sharply upward during the latter half of the 1960s. The number of households on the welfare rolls stood at 800,000 in 1960 and 1 million in 1965. Then, in just the five short years thereafter, the number more than doubled to 2.5 million by 1970. It continued to climb to 3.3 million in 1975.

51. Charles Murray, *Losing Ground: American Social Policy, 1950–1980* (New York: Basic Books, 1984), pp. 53–133, and "Does Welfare Bring More Babies?," *The American Enterprise*, vol. 5, no. 1 (January/February 1994): pp. 52–59.

52. For the growth rates of teenage illegitimacy, see note 35.

53. The pathbreaking study here is David Ellwood and Mary Jo Bane, "The Impact of AFDC on Family Structure and Living Arrangements," in R. Ehrenberg, ed., *Research in Labor Economics*, vol. 7 (Greenwich, Conn.: JAI Press, 1985), pp. 137–207; a survey of results of other studies in the area is found in Robert D. Plotnick, "The Effect of Social Policies on Teenage Pregnancy and Childbearing," *Families in Society*, vol. 74, no. 6 (June 1993): pp. 324–28.

54. The basic welfare package includes AFDC payments, food stamps, and Medicaid. Housing assistance goes to only about one third of families on welfare. In Connecticut, the state with the highest benefits, AFDC and food stamps together amounted to a maximum of $10,464 a year in 1994 for a three-person family. Counting Medicaid as worth $2,000, the total came to $12,464. The after-tax base-line income in 1994 for such a household was slightly more than $18,000. Figures on benefits are from the office of Family Assistance of the United States Department of Health and Human Services and from the Congressional Research Service.

55. AFDC, food stamps, and Medicaid (valued at $2,000) in the state with the lowest benefits (Mississippi) for a household of three came to $7,030 in 1994. The state with the highest benefits in the continental United States (Connecticut) provided $12,464 in 1994, or 79 percent more. Figures are from the Office of Family Assistance of the United States Department of Health and Human Services and from the Congressional Research Service.

56. Charles Murray, "Welfare and the Family: The U.S. Experience," *Journal of Labor Economics*, vol. 2, no. 1 (1993): pp. S247–53. The correlations Murray finds for whites after 1965 (generally in the range of .35) would account for 12 percent of illegitimacy (see p. S248). He found no correlation for blacks (p. S250).

57. The five states with the lowest benefit levels were Alabama, Louisiana, Mississippi, Tennessee, and Texas. Data on benefit levels are from the Office of Family Assistance of the United States Department of Health and Human Services and from the Congressional Research Service. Counting Medicaid as worth $2,000, benefits in all five states (including AFDC, food stamps, and Medicaid) in 1994 for a family of three ranged from $7,030 to $7,990. The poverty line for a household of three in 1994 was about $12,000 a year.

58. Murray, *Losing Ground*, pp. 157–59.

59. Besharov, "Born to Lose," p. 24.

60. *Report of the National Advisory Commission on Civil Disorders*, 1968, pp. 132–33, 175. Surveys in places like Richmond, California, in 1964 reveal sizable minorities of both white and black youth perceived an absence of opportunity (see Chapter 5, pages 81–82).

61. Richard B. Freeman, "Crime and the Employment of Disadvantaged Youths," in George E. Peterson and Wayne Vroman, eds., *Urban Labor Markets and Job Opportunity* (Washington, D.C.: Urban Institute Press, 1992), p. 231.

62. Jay MacLeod, *Ain't No Makin It: Aspirations and Attainment in a Low-Income Neighborhood* (Boulder, Colo.: Westview Press, 1995) p. 72.

63. Freeman, "Crime and the Employment of Disadvantaged Youths," in Peterson and Vroman, *Urban Labor Markets*, pp. 229–30. The survey took place among youths living in Boston.

64. Quoted in "Parents' Jobs Key to Success of Inner-city Kids," *Arizona Daily Star*, March 24, 1994, p. 16A.

65. George E. Peterson and Wayne Vroman, "Urban Labor Markets and Economic Opportunity," in Peterson and Vroman, *Urban Labor Markets*, pp. 20–21.

66. See C. R. Huff, "Young Gangs and Public Policy," *Crime and Delinquency*, vol. 35 (1989): pp. 524–37; Emilie Andersen Allan and Darrell J. Steffensmeier, "Youth, Underemployment, and Property Crime: Differential Effects of Job Availability and Job Quality on Juvenile and Young Adult Arrest Rates," *American Sociological Review*, vol. 54 (February 1989): pp. 107–23; W. Kip Viscusi, "Market Incentives for Criminal Behavior," in Richard Freeman and Harry J. Holzer, eds., *The Black Youth Employment Crisis* (Chicago: University of Chicago Press, 1986), pp. 301–46; and Isaac Erlich, "Participation in Illegitimate Activities: An Economic Analysis," in Gary S. Becker and William M. Landes, eds., *Essays in the Economics of Crime and Punishment* (New York: Columbia University Press, 1974), pp. 68–134.

67. Rustin is quoted earlier, p. 113.

68. R Baird Shuman, "Big Guns, Thwarted Dreams: School Violence and the English Teacher," *English Journal*, vol. 84, no. 5 (September 1995): pp. 24–25.

69. Quoted in Vern E. Smith et al., "Children of the Underclass," *Newsweek*, September 11, 1989, p. 20.

70. Allan and Steffensmeier, "Youth, Unemployment, and Property Crime," p. 115, Table 2.

71. *Statistical Abstract of the United States, 1992*, p. 197, Table 330.

72. Ibid., p. 180, Table 287. The crime rate was 5,950 per 100,000 population in 1980 and 5,820 per 100,000 population in 1990. The rate did decline from 1980 to 1984, to 5,031 per 100,000 population, but rose again thereafter, to 5,820 per 100,000 in 1990. The rate was 1,516 per 100,000 population in 1965.

73. Christopher Jencks, *Rethinking Social Policy: Race, Poverty, and the Underclass* (New York: HarperCollins, 1992), p. 109.

74. Barbara Dafoe Whitehead, "Dan Quayle Was Right," *Atlantic Monthly,* April 1993, p. 77.

75. See pages 111–16 of this chapter.

76. Sara S. McLanahan, "The Consequences of Single Motherhood," *The American Prospect,* no. 18 (Summer 1994): pp. 51–53.

Chapter 8

1. William H. Flanigan and Nancy H. Zingale, *Political Behavior of the American Electorate,* 8th ed. (Washington, D.C.: Congressional Quarterly Press, 1994), p. 63, Table 3-2.

2. On the importance that Republicans attached to both economic independence and a Homestead Act, see Eric Foner, *Free Soil, Free Labor, Free Men: The Ideology of the Republican Party Before the Civil War* (New York: Oxford University Press, 1970), esp. pp. 27–31.

3. For the 1860 platform of the Republican party, see Kirk Harold Porter, *National Party Platforms, 1840–1968* (Urbana, Ill.: University of Illinois Press, 1970), pp. 31–33.

4. Ronald Reagan, "Inaugural Address," in Ellis Sandoz and Cecil V. Crabb, Jr., eds, *A Tide of Discontent* (Washington, D.C.: Congressional Quarterly Press, 1981), p. 212. See also the Reagan Program for Economic Recovery, "Program for Economic Recovery, White House Report, February 19, 1981," *Weekly Compilation of Presidential Documents,* vol. 17, no. 8 (1981): p. 141: "The most important cause of our economic problems has been the government itself. The Federal Government, through tax, spending, regulation, and monetary policies, has sacrificed long-term growth and price stability for ephemeral short-term goals."

5. "Dole Opens Third Presidential Bid, Calls Clinton a 'Clever Apologist,'" *Arizona Daily Star,* April 11, 1995, p. A3.

6. "Candidates Court Perot Supporters," *Arizona Daily Star*, August 13, 1995, p. A4.

7. "Republican Forbes Formally Enters Race," *Arizona Daily Star*, September 23, 1995, p. 3A.

8. Cited in William Raspberry, "Blather on Both Sides," *Washington Post National Weekly Edition*, May 6–12, 1996, p. 26.

9. Milton Friedman and Rose Friedman, *Free to Choose* (New York: Avon, 1979), pp. 106–10.

10. Figures for total federal expenditures, excluding Social Security and Medicare, and the GNP (in parentheses) were $64.0 billion ($405.9 billion) in 1955; $80.6 billion ($515.3 billion) in 1960; $440.3 billion ($2,732.0 billion) in 1980; and $905.1 billion ($5,513.8 billion) in 1990. Data on federal expenditures can be found in *Statistical Abstract of the United States, 1992*, p. 317, Table 494, p. 318, Table 495, data on the GNP back to 1959 can be found in *Economic Report of the President, 1986*, p. 252, Table B-1; and for 1955 in *Economic Report of the President, 1992*, p. 298, Table B-1. State and local spending, too, remained steady at just over 12.5 percent of the GNP both in 1970 and 1990. Data on state and local expenditures are in *Economic Report of the President, 1992*, p. 392, Table BN-80.

11. Figures for total federal tax receipts, excluding social insurance receipts, and the GNP (in parentheses) were $75.1 billion ($515.3 billion) in 1960 and $603.1 billion ($5,513.8 billion) in 1990. Data on federal tax receipts and social insurance contributions can be found in *Economic Report of the President, 1992*, p. 389, Table B-77, p. 390, Table B-78. Sources for GNP data are cited in note 10. Total federal tax receipts exclusive of social insurance receipts came to 12.3 percent of the GNP in 1980, just prior to the Reagan presidency, and to 10.8 percent and 10.6 percent of the GNP in 1983 and 1984.

12. As for the effect of the tax reductions on prosperity through the resulting enlarged debt (the total federal debt grew from less than 40 percent to more than 50 percent of the GNP from 1980 to 1990), it is well to recall that in 1950, when the nation was about to experience a golden age of prosperity, the total federal debt relative to the GNP was larger by half than at any time during the 1990s.

13. Robert W. Hahn and Thomas D. Hopkins, "Regulation/Deregulation: Looking Backward, Looking Forward," *The American Enterprise*, vol. 3 (July/August 1992): p. 73.

14. Ibid., in 1979 dollars.

15. $328 billion in 1990 was 0.6 percent less of the GNP than $290 billion in 1979, which the study says was spent in 1990 dollars in 1979.

16. The growth of regulatory costs from 1974 through 1979 is examined in John E. Schwarz, *America's Hidden Success: A Reassessment of Public Policy from Kennedy to Reagan* (New York: W. W. Norton, 1987), pp. 90–99, based on data from Murray L. Weidenbaum, "The Costs of Government Regulation of Business," Joint Economic Committee, U.S. Congress, April 10, 1978, p. 16; and Murray L. Weidenbaum, *The Future of Government Regulation* (New York: Amacom, 1979), p. 23.

17. Bryan T. Johnson and Thomas P. Sheehy, *The Index of Economic Freedom* (Washington, D.C.: Heritage Foundation, 1995). A list of the criteria is on pp. 11–21; a list of the overall results is on pp. 249–51.

18. Ibid., p. 249.

19. Schwarz, *America's Hidden Success*, pp. 61–68, esp. p. 67; and the U.S. Department of Labor, *Handbook of Labor Statistics*, August 1989, bulletin no. 2340, p. 348, Table 98; p. 358, Table 101.

20. An overview of a diversity of approaches and their findings is contained in George W. Downs and Patrick D. Larkey, *The Search for Government Efficiency: From Hubris to Helplessness* (New York: Random House, 1986), pp. 30–40.

21. Friedman and Friedman, *Free to Choose*, p. 99.

22. Ibid.

23. *Statistical Abstract of the United States, 1982–83*, p. 319, Table 517. The figure on government spending includes federal, state, and local expenditures.

24. Consider the case of a family of four that receives $10,000 in benefits while earning $5,000, bringing the family to a $15,000 poverty-line income. If working longer hours and earning $10,000 would reduce governmental support to $5,000, thereby leaving the family at the same $15,000 income, there would be no material benefit to working longer hours. To retain incentive, assistance would need to be available even to households that had passed the poverty line. If, to avoid this, the benefits were scaled down to zero by the time the poverty line was reached, the programs would then lift very few families up to the poverty line. For example, were benefits set to total one half of the difference between family earnings and the poverty line, no household would be lifted above the poverty line and, indeed, none would be lifted to the poverty line itself.

25. For a more recent illustration of the same fallacies the Friedmans fell into, see columnist Walter Williams, "The Result of Welfare in Modern-Day Slavery," *Post and Courier* (Charleston, S.C.), November 22, 1995, p. 13-A.

26. Daniel Schorr, "Washington Notebook," *The New Leader*, March 13–27, 1995, p. 3.

27. Michael Kinsley, "The Intellectual Free Lunch: Everybody's Entitled to an Opinion, Right? Wrong," *The New Yorker*, February 6, 1995, pp. 4–5.

28. On the computer and jet airplane industries, see Richard R. Nelson, *High-Technology Policies: A Five-Nation Comparison* (Washington, D.C.: American Enterprise Institute, 1984), pp. 42–65.

29. Ibid.

30. Steven Thomma, "View Spreading of Government as the Enemy," *Arizona Daily Star*, April 30, 1995, pp. A1, A6.

Chapter 9

1. Gertrude Himmelfarb, *The De-Moralization of Society: From Victorian Virtues to Modern Values* (New York: Alfred A. Knopf, 1995), p. 9.

2. Ibid., p. 15.

3. See Chapter 7 for evidence.

4. Quoted in Bob Herbert, "A Reckless Journey," *New York Times*, January 4, 1995, p. A19.

5. Peter J. Boyer, "Looking for Justice in L.A.," *The New Yorker*, March 15, 1993, p. 80.

6. Michael Kelly, "The Man of the Minute," *The New Yorker*, July 17, 1995, p. 27.

7. Newt Gingrich, "Renewing America," *Newsweek*, July 10, 1995, pp. 26–27.

8. See Chapter 8.

9. See Chapter 8.

10. See Chapter 5.

11. From data published in "The Trouble with Success," *The Economist*, March 12, 1994, p. 78, Table 1.

12. The amount of work required allowing most heads of household to gain independence from the typical small farm in the era of the founders took an amount of time that generally would not have exceeded the two thousand hours of work demanded today in a job occupying forty hours a week over fifty-two weeks of the year. The work might well be more time-consuming in some stretches, especially during early spring or late summer, but less so at other times, such as in the winter. Independence was a condition that the common person, with an ordinary level of skill and energy, ought to have been able to attain, not just people with extraordinary skills or exceptional levels of energy. See Chapter 2, pp. 25–26.

13. The percentages applying to distressed workers are somewhat lower than those pertaining to the shortfall in adequate jobs partly because the denominator of the former is based on all workers in the labor force rather than simply households and because its numerator does not incorporate discouraged workers—those workers who have dropped out of the labor market altogether due to lack of success (the number of these workers, probably over a million, is hard to estimate).

14. See Chapter 5, note 32.

15. See Chapter 6, pp. 93–94, and Chapter 8.

16. See note 35 below and page 95.

17. Richard B. Freeman, "How Much De-unionization Contributed to the Rise in Male Earnings Inequality," in Sheldon Danziger and Peter Gottschalk, eds., *Uneven Tides: Rising Inequality in America* (New York: Russell Sage Foundation, 1993), pp. 158–59.

18. Thomas J. Volgy, John E. Schwarz, and Lawrence E. Imwalle, "In Search of Economic Well-being: The Relation Between Worker Power and Economic Returns in Ten Industrial Nations," *American Journal of Political Science*, vol. 40, no. 4 (November 1996): pp. 1233–53.

19. Lawrence Mishel and David M. Frankel, *The State of Working America, 1990–91* (Armonk, N.Y.: M. E. Sharpe, 1991), p. 114, Table 3.34.

20. Alternative models of worker participation and codetermination are described in Jeff Rogers and Wolfgang Steek, "Workplace Representation Overseas: The Works Councils Story," in Richard B. Freeman, ed., *Working Under Different Rules* (New York: Russell Sage Foundation, 1993), pp. 97–156.

21. The argument will be made that raising the minimum wage leads to job losses, especially with respect to entry-level jobs, in the cases of employers unable to afford paying the higher minimum wage. The evidence is very mixed about this assertion; the totality of this mixed evidence suggests that the impact is small. For a review of the evidence from recent studies, see John Kennan, "The Elusive Effects of Minimum Wages," *Journal of Economic Literature*, vol. 30, no. 4 (December 1995): pp. 1949–65.

22. This is in 1994 dollars. Appendix B discusses the issue of whether persons who receive assistance from the government in the form of subsidies to wages, public-sector jobs, or jobs created through government incentives can be considered to be "independent."

23. A 12 percent phaseout rate after the maximum of $4,700 has been reached would result in a marginal tax rate of 35 percent, including both income and Social Security taxes. The projected costs of this program, reviewed later in the chapter, take into account the new $4,700 maximum and a 12 percent phaseout rate.

24. The number of employed rose from 85 million to 125 million from 1973 to 1995, a 47 percent increase over those twenty-two years.

25. As indicated in Chapter 5, demand for new adequate jobs can be expected to increase at about 1.1 million a year. A 2 percent increase a year in jobs will produce about 2.6 million net new jobs a year in total, including 1.6 million adequate jobs, or a surplus of 500,000 relative to new demand.

26. Robert H. Haveman and John Karl Scholz, "The Clinton Welfare Reform Plan: Will It End Poverty as We Know It?," *Focus*, vol. 16, no. 2 (Winter 1994/95): p. 8 (pp. 1–11); see also John Bishop and Robert Haveman, "Selective Employment Subsidies: Can Okun's Law Be Repealed?," *American Economic Review*, vol. 69 (May 1979): pp. 124–30; and Jeffrey M. Perloff and Michael L. Wachter, "The New Jobs Tax Credit: An Evaluation of the 1977–1978 Wage Subsidy Program," *American Economic Review*, vol. 69 (May 1979): pp. 173–79.

27. Baltimore, Milwaukee, and Santa Clara County in California have experimented with this approach. See Louis Uchitelle, "From Government Cash to a New Living Wage," *Beacon Journal*, April 9, 1996, pp. A1, A4.

28. Paul Offner, "How Workfare Can Work," *The New Republic*, March 14, 1994, pp. 17–18. President Clinton suggests that the government can play an important role in providing jobs to families now on welfare by giving them priority when hiring for current jobs. A problem here is that these jobs then are not available to the others who would have gotten them, forcing them to have to remain unemployed or turn to welfare. Few of these jobs are available in any case. In the case of entry-level positions, one estimate finds that in 1996 the federal government hired for fewer than 120 permanent blue-collar jobs in the areas of Boston, New York City, Dallas, and Seattle, combined. See Bob Herbert, "The Artful Dodger," *New York Times*, March 10, 1997.

29. Among the factors affecting feasibility is the income of the nonresident father, which evidence indicates is less than $5,000 annually for between 15 and 25 percent of them. See Judith A. Seltzer and Daniel R. Meyer, "Child Support and Children's Well-being," *Focus*, vol. 17, no. 3 (Spring 1996): p. 34.

30. The official standard for full-time employment is 1,750 hours a year.

31. The phaseout tax rate on the public money is similar to the 12 percent for the EITC.

32. Some reduction from annual full-time hours, for a reasonable period of time, will have to be made to take account of considerations such as circumstances that require child care from the single parent or unemployment that is beyond the individual's control.

33. As Chapter 4 indicates, $2,000 a year is already contained in the household budget.

34. Growth in years of education slowed dramatically after 1970. The average educational level of American adults was 9.3 years in 1950; 10.6 years in 1960; 12.1 years in 1970; 12.5 years in 1980; and 12.7 years in 1990. See the *Statistical Abstract of the United States, 1993*, p. 152, Table 230.

35. *Net* nonresidential investment averaged 3.6 percent of the GNP annually in the 1960s and 3.8 percent of GNP annually in the 1970s. The falloff in the rate of growth of the amount of capital per worker since 1970 has primarily been due to the precipitous increase in the number of workers, not to a decline in investment.

36. A discussion of school-to-work vocational philosophies, literature, and some experimental programs in the United States may be found in Susan Goldberger and Richard Kazis, "Revitalizing High Schools: What the School-to-Career Movement Can Contribute," *Phi Delta Kappan*, April 1996, pp. 547–54 and Michael Hartoonian and Richard Van Scotter, "School-to-Work: A Model for Learning and Living," *Phi Delta Kappan*, April 1996, pp. 555–60.

37. Eileen Applebaum and Rosemary Batt, *The New American Workplace*

(Ithaca, N.Y.: Cornell University Press, 1994), p. 40. On the German apprenticeship system and how it is funded, see also John R. McKernan, Jr., *Making the Grade* (Boston: Little, Brown, 1994).

38. David I. Levine and Laura D'Andrea Tyson, "Participation, Productivity, and the Firm's Environment," in Alan Blinder, ed., *Paying for Productivity* (Washington, D.C.: Brookings Institution, 1990), pp. 183–206.

39. Rogers and Steek, "Workplace Representation Overseas," pp. 104–10.

40. David I. Levine, *Reinventing the Workplace: How Business and Employees Can Both Win* (Washington, D.C.: Brookings Institution, 1995), p. 83. Even if workers' participation had little effect on productivity, it would remain right for employers to provide an appropriate place for the voice of workers to be heard in a society committed to the idea of equal respect.

41. A tax of three quarters of 1 percent would produce this amount.

42. The estimated revenues include both the employee's and the employer's share.

43. The position of Richard J. Herrnstein and Charles A. Murray in their book, *The Bell Curve: Intelligence and Structure in American Life* (New York: Free Press, 1994), indicates the profound resonance among many conservatives of the idea that people with little or no opportunity, but who practice the work ethic, deserve the help of the community to be able to live decently. They conclude:

"The evidence about cognitive ability causes us to be sympathetic to the straightforward proposition that "trying hard" ought to be rewarded.... People who work full time should not be too poor to have a decent standard of living, even if the kinds of work they can do are not highly valued in the marketplace....

"How? There is no economically perfect alternative. Any government supplement of wages produces negative effects of many kinds. Such defects are not the results of bad policy but inherent. The least damaging strategies are the simplest ones, which do not try to oversee or manipulate the labor-market behavior of low-income people, but rather augment their earned income up to a floor. The earned income tax credit, already in place, seems to be a generally good strategy, albeit with the unavoidable drawbacks of any income supplement."

The chief issue, they say, "is how to redistribute in ways that increase the chances for people at the bottom of society to take control of their lives, to be engaged meaningfully in their communities, and to find valued places for themselves."

The quotes are from Herrnstein and Murray, *The Bell Curve*, pp. 547–48.

Appendix A

1. Katharine G. Abraham, "Structural/Frictional vs. Deficient Demand Unemployment: Some New Evidence," *American Economic Review*, vol. 73 (September–December 1983): pp. 708–24.

2. Ibid., p. 713, Table 1, under point 6.

3. Three months or so as compared to two weeks.

4. 6.2 million unemployed workers divided by 7.5 equals 830,000.

5. Five days is 1/73 year; multiplying 830,000 times 73 equals 60.5 million.

6. Abraham, "Structural/Frictional vs. Deficient Demand Unemployment," p. 121, Table 4, shows that for January 1973, when unemployment was 5.5 percent, the unemployment-vacancy ratio was 3.8, assuming a ten-calendar-day mean vacancy duration. Unemployment for January 1968 was 4.0 with an unemployment-vacancy ratio of 1.3, assuming a five-calendar-day mean vacancy duration. For 1989, unemployment was 5.2 percent for which I have assigned an unemployment-vacancy ratio of 3.3.

7. See Ibid., p. 721. Abraham associated an unemployment rate nearest to 5.2 percent (the 5.5 percent unemployment rate of January 1973) with a mean vacancy duration of ten calendar days.

8. Total receipts of 75 percent of all nonfarm proprietorships and 60 percent of all partnerships fall below $25,000 a year. See *Statistical Abstract of the United States, 1992*, p. 519, Table 826.

Appendix C

1. There are rare exceptions regarding a few individual items in the yearly family budgets. In the 1989 budget, for example, the cost of operating a car had to be calculated from 1988 figures. I then adjusted the cost by the rise in consumer prices for transportation from 1988 to 1989. The large majority of prices in the budgets are current-year prices, however. Even the few exceptions derive from the prices of a nearby year.

2. See Chapter 6, pp. 91–92, and note 11.

ACKNOWLEDGMENTS

This book owes much to the help of many people. Among my colleagues and friends at the University of Arizona and elsewhere, I gratefully acknowledge the contributions of Allen Buchanan, Tom Christiano, Richard Cosgrove, Elizabeth Ervin, Gordon Fuller, Michael Gottfredson, Jody Glittenberg, Travis Hirschi, Lee Kane, Barbara Kingsolver, Keith Lehrer, Jack Marietta, Doug McAdam, Cary Nederman, Jim Todd, and Tom Volgy. I owe a large debt to each of them. Each and every page of the book has benefited from their assistance and I personally from their inspiration and unyielding support. I also have had the aid of extraordinary students and staff: Nicole Ewing, Sally Garnaat, Donna Kelley, A. J. Marston, Trisha Morris, and Loretta Sowers. To my editor, Alane Mason, I express my deep respect and appreciation not only for her efforts on behalf of the book but also for her remarkable gifts of language. Ashley Barnes answered all my questions not simply with competence but with immense grace and patience, for which I am ever thankful. I have been fortunate to have the advice and support of Roby Harrington, longtime valued friend, who has always been there when needed. Finally, my profound gratitude and everlasting appreciation goes to my loving wife, Judi, as well as to my children, Jodi, Jennifer, and Laurie, for everything they have given me.

SELECTED BIBLIOGRAPHY

Abraham, Katherine G. "Structural/Frictional vs. Deficient Demand Unemployment: Some New Evidence." *American Economic Review*, vol. 73 (September–December, 1983).

Akerlof, George A., and Janet L. Yellen. *Efficiency Wage Models of the Labor Market*. Cambridge: Cambridge University Press, 1986.

Alford, C. Fred. *Group Psychology and Political Theory*. New Haven, Conn.: Yale University Press, 1994.

Allan, Emilie Andersen, and Darrell J. Steffensmeier. "Youth, Underemployment, and Property Crime: Differential Effects of Job Availability and Job Quality on Juvenile and Young Adult Arrest Rates." *American Sociological Review*, vol. 4 (February 1989).

Anderson, Elijah. "Sex Codes and Family Life Among Poor Inner-City Youths." *Annals of the American Academy of Political and Social Science*, vol. 501 (January 1989).

Angell, Roger. "Two Dreams." *The New Yorker*, March 13, 1995.

Applebaum, Eileen, and Rosemary Batt. *The New American Workplace*. Ithaca, N.Y.: Cornell University Press, 1994.

Armor, David. *Forced Justice.* New York: Oxford University Press, 1995.

Aronson, Robert L. *Self-employment: A Labor Market Perspective.* Ithaca, N.Y.: ILR Press, 1991.

Axelrod, Robert. *The Evolution of Cooperation.* New York: Basic Books, 1984.

Bailyn, Bernard. *The Ideological Origins of the American Revolution.* Cambridge, Mass.: Harvard University Press, 1967.

Bane, Mary Jo. "Welfare Reform and Mandatory Versus Voluntary Work." *Journal of Policy Analysis and Management,* vol. 8 (1989).

Barry, Brian. *Democracy, Power, and Justice.* Oxford, England: Clarendon Press, 1989.

Baumol, William J., et al. *Productivity and American Leadership: The Long View.* Cambridge, Mass.: MIT Press, 1989.

Becker, Gary S. "Family Economics and Macro Behavior." *American Economic Review,* vol. 78, no. 1 (March 1988).

Bell, Carolyn S. *The Economics of the Ghetto.* New York: Pegasus, 1970.

Bellah, Robert N., et al. *The Good Society.* New York: Vintage Books, 1991.

Bennett, William J. *The Moral Compass.* New York: Simon and Schuster, 1995.

Berlin, Gordon, and Andrew Sum. *Toward a More Perfect Union: Basic Skills, Poor Families and Our Economic Future.* New York: Ford Foundation, 1988.

Besharov, Douglas J. "Born to Lose: Welfare Reform Will Work Only If It Addresses the Problem of Out-of-Wedlock Births." *Washington Post National Weekly Edition,* December 20–26, 1993.

———. "Not All Single Mothers Are Created Equal." *The American Enterprise,* vol. 3, no. 5 (September/October 1992).

———, and Karen N. Gardiner. "Truth and Consequences: Teen Sex." *The American Enterprise,* January–February 1993.

Bishop, John, and Robert Haveman. "Selective Employment Subsidies: Can Okun's Law Be Repealed?" *American Economic Review,* vol. 69 (May 1979).

Blank, Rebecca M. "Are Part-Time Jobs Bad Jobs?" In Gary Burtless, ed., *A Future of Lousy Jobs?* Washington, D.C.: Brookings Institution, 1990.

Bosworth, Barry, and George L. Perry. "Productivity and Real Wages: Is There a Puzzle?" *Brookings Papers on Economic Activity,* vol. 1 (1994). Washington, D.C.: Brookings Institution, 1994.

Borjas, George J. *Friends and Strangers: The Impact of Immigrants in the U.S. Economy.* New York: Basic Books, 1990.

Boyd, Julian P. *The Declaration of Independence: The Evolution of the Text as Shown in Facsimiles of Various Drafts by Its Author, Thomas Jefferson.* Princeton, N.J.: Princeton University Press, 1945.

Boyer, Peter J. "Looking for Justice in L.A." *The New Yorker,* March 15, 1993.

Bracey, Gerald W. "The Assessor Assessed: A 'Revisionist' Looks at a Critique of the Sandia Report." *Journal of Educational Research,* vol. 88, no. 3 (January/February, 1995).

Bragg, Rick. "Big Holes Where the Dignity Used to Be." *New York Times,* March 5, 1996.

Buchanan, Allen. "Justice as Reciprocity Versus Subject-Centered Justice." *Philosophy and Public Affairs,* vol. 19, no. 3 (Summer 1990).

Burtless, Gary. "Earnings Inequalities over the Business Cycles." In Gary Burtless, ed., *A Future of Lousy Jobs?: The Changing Structure of U.S. Wages.* Washington, D.C.: Brookings Institution, 1990.

Chandler, Clay. "Is It Half Empty, or Half Full?" *Washington Post National Weekly Edition,* July 29–August 4, 1996.

Chira, Susan. "Care at Most Child Day Centers Rated as Poor." *New York Times,* February 7, 1995.

Christensen, Bryce, et al. *The Family Wage: Work, Gender, and Children in the Modern Economy.* Rockford, Ill.: Rockford Institute, 1988.

Condit, Celeste Michelle, and John Louis Lucaites. *Crafting Equality: America's Anglo-African Word.* Chicago: University of Chicago Press, 1993.

Congressional Budget Office. "In Pursuit of Higher Wages and Employment-Based Health Insurance." February 1993.

Cramer, J. C. "Employment Trends of Young Mothers and the Opportunity Costs of Babies in the United States." *Demography,* vol. 16 (1979).

Danziger, Sheldon, and Peter Gottschalk. *America Unequal.* Cambridge, Mass.: Harvard University Press, 1995.

———, et al. "The Direct Measurement of Welfare Levels: How Much Does It Cost to Make Ends Meet?" *Review of Economics and Statistics,* vol. 66, no. 3 (1984).

Davis, David Brion. *Revolutions: Reflections on American Equality and Foreign Liberation.* Cambridge, Mass.: Harvard University Press, 1990.

De Parle, Jason. "When Giving Up Welfare for a Job Just Doesn't Pay." *New York Times*, July 8, 1992.

Demning, W. Edwards. *Out of the Crisis*. Cambridge, Mass.: Massachusetts Institute of Technology Press, 1982.

Denison, Edward F. *Why Growth Rates Differ: Postwar Experience in Nine Western Countries*. Washington, D. C.: Brookings Institution, 1967.

Downs, George W., and Patrick D. Larkey. *The Search for Government Efficiency: From Hubris to Helplessness*. New York: Random House, 1986.

Duncan, Greg J., and Saul D. Hoffman. "Welfare Benefits, Economic Opportunities, and Out-of-Wedlock Births Among Teenage Girls." *Demography*, vol. 27, no. 4 (November 1990).

Dunlop, John. "The Task of Contemporary Wage Theory." In John Dunlop, ed., *The Theory of Wage Determination*. New York: St. Martin's Press, 1957.

Dworkin, Ronald. *Taking Rights Seriously*. Cambridge, Mass.: Harvard University Press, 1977.

Ellwood, David, and Mary Jo Bane. "The Impact of AFDC on Family Structure and Living Arrangements." In R. Ehrenberg, ed., *Research in Labor Economics*, vol. 7 (Greenwich, Conn.: JAI Press, 1985).

————, *Poor Support: Poverty and the American Family*. New York: Basic Books, 1988.

Erlich, Isaac. "Participation in Illegitimate Activities: An Economic Analysis." In Gary S. Becker and William M. Landes, eds., *Essays in the Economics of Crime and Punishment*. New York: Columbia University Press, 1974.

Farber, Naomi B. "The Significance of Aspirations Among Unmarried Adolescent Mothers." *Social Service Review*, December 1989.

The Federalist. New York: Random House, Modern Library.

Flanigan, William H., and Nancy H. Zingale. *Political Behavior of the American Electorate*. 8th ed. Washington, D.C.: Congressional Quarterly Press, 1994.

Foner, Eric. *Free Soil, Free Labor, Free Men: The Ideology of the Republican Party Before the Civil War*. New York: Oxford University Press, 1970.

Freeman, Richard B. "Crime and the Employment of Disadvantaged Youths." In George E. Peterson and Wayne Vroman, eds., *Urban Labor Markets and Job Opportunity*. Washington, D.C.: Urban Institute Press, 1992.

————. "How Much De-unionization Contributed to the Rise in Male

Earnings Inequality." In Sheldon Danziger and Peter Gottschalk, eds., *Uneven Tides: Rising Inequality in America*. New York: Russell Sage Foundation, 1993.

———, ed. *Working Under Different Rules*. New York: Russell Sage Foundation, 1994.

———, and Harry J. Holzer, eds. *The Black Youth Employment Crisis*. Chicago: University of Chicago Press, 1986.

Friedlander, Daniel, and Gary Burtless. *Five Years After: The Long-term Effects of Welfare-to-Work Programs*. New York: Russell Sage Foundation, 1995.

Friedman, Milton, and Rose Friedman. *Free to Choose*. New York: Avon, 1979.

Frum, David. *Dead Right*. New York: Basic Books, 1994.

Funk, Robert W., et al. (The Jesus Seminar). *The Five Gospels: The Search for the Authentic Words of Jesus*. New York: Macmillan, 1995.

Furstenberg, Frank, Jr. "As the Pendulum Swings: Teenage Childbearing and Social Concern." *Family Relations*, vol. 40, no. 2 (April 1991).

Garson, Barbara. *The Electronic Sweatshop: How Computers Are Transforming the Office of the Future into the Factory of the Past*. New York: Penguin, 1988.

Geronimus, Arline T. "Teenage Childbearing and Social and Reproductive Disadvantage: The Evolution of Complex Questions and the Demise of Simple Answers." *Family Relations*, vol. 40 (October 1991).

———, and Sanders Korenman. "The Socioeconomic Consequences of Teen Childbearing Reconsidered." *Quarterly Journal of Economics*, vol. 107, no. 4 (November 1992).

Gibbs, Nancy. "The Vicious Cycle." *Time*, June 20, 1994.

Gilbert, Dennis A. *Compendium of American Public Opinion*. New York: Facts on File Publications, 1988.

Gingrich, Newt. "Renewing America." *Newsweek*, July 10, 1995.

Goldberger, Susan, and Richard Kazis. "Revitalizing High Schools: What the School-to-Career Movement Can Contribute." *Phi Delta Kappan*, April 1996.

Goodwin, Leonard. *Causes and Cures of Welfare: New Evidence on the Social Psychology of the Poor*. Boston: Lexington Books, 1983.

———. *Do the Poor Want to Work?: A Social-Psychological Study of Work Orientations*. Washington, D.C.: Brookings Institution, 1972.

Greeley, Horace. "An Address to the Printers of New York." January 17, 1850.

Greene, Jack P. *All Men Are Created Equal: Some Reflections on the Character of the American Revolution. An inaugural lecture delivered before the University of Oxford on February 10, 1976.* Oxford: Clarendon Press, 1976.

Gueron, Judith M., and Edward Pauly. *From Welfare to Work: A Summary.* New York: Russell Sage Foundation, 1991.

Gutmann, Amy, ed. *Democracy and the Welfare State.* Princeton, N.J.: Princeton University Press, 1988.

Hahn, Robert W., and Thomas D. Hopkins. "Regulation/Deregulation: Looking Backward, Looking Forward." *The American Enterprise*, vol. 3 (July/August 1992).

Handler, Joel F. *The Poverty of Welfare Reform.* New Haven, Conn.: Yale University Press, 1995.

Hanson, Sandra L., David E. Meyers, and Alan L. Ginsburg. "The Role of Responsibility and Knowledge in Reducing Teenage Out-of-Wedlock Childbearing." *Journal of Marriage and Family*, vol. 49, no. 2 (May 1987).

Harrington, Michael. *The Other America: Poverty in the United States.* New York: Macmillan, 1962.

Hartoonian, Michael, and Richard Van Scotter. "School-to-Work: A Model for Learning and Living." *Phi Delta Kappan*, April 1996.

Haveman, Robert. "From Welfare to Work: Problems and Pitfalls." *Focus*, vol. 18, no. 1 (special issue, 1996).

———, and John Karl Schloz. "The Clinton Welfare Reform Plan: Will It End Poverty as We Know It?" *Focus*, vol. 16, no. 2 (Winter 1994/95).

Hayek, Friedrich A. *The Constitution of Liberty.* Chicago: University of Chicago Press, 1960.

———. *Law, Legislation and Liberty.* Chicago: University of Chicago Press, 1976.

———. *The Road to Serfdom.* Chicago: University of Chicago Press, 1960.

Herbert, Bob. "A Reckless Journey." *New York Times*, January 4, 1995.

Herrnstein, Richard J., and Charles A. Murray. *The Bell Curve: Intelligence and Class Structure in American Life.* New York: Free Press, 1994.

Himmelfarb, Gertrude. *The De-Moralization of Society: From Victorian Virtues to Modern Values.* New York: Alfred A. Knopf, 1995.

———. *The Idea of Poverty: England in the Early Industrial Age.* New York: Random House, 1983.

Hochschild, Jennifer L. "The Double-Edged Sword of Equal Opportunity." In Ian Shapiro and Grant Reeher, eds., *Power, Inequality, and Democratic Politics: Essays in Honor of Robert A. Dahl*. Boulder, Colo.: Westview Press, 1988.

———. "The Political Contingency of Public Opinion, or What Shall We Make of the Declining Faith of Middle-Class African Americans?" *PS: Political Science and Politics*, vol. 27, no. 1 (March 1994).

Hogan, D. P., and E. M. Kitagawa. "The Impact of Social Status, Family Structure, and Neighborhood on the Fertility of Black Adolescents." *American Journal of Sociology*, vol. 90, no. 4 (1985).

Horwitz, Tony. "Minimum Wage Jobs Give Many Americans Only a Miserable Life." *Wall Street Journal*, November 12, 1993.

———. "The Six Growth Jobs Are Dull, Dead-End, Sometimes Dangerous." *Wall Street Journal*, December 1, 1994.

Howard, A. E. Dick. "For the Common Benefit: The Virginia Declaration of Rights of 1776." *The George Mason Lectures: Honoring the Two Hundredth Anniversary of the Virginia Declaration of Rights*. Williamsburg, June 12, 1976.

Huff, C. R. "Young Gangs and Public Policy." *Crime and Delinquency*, vol. 35 (1989).

Hulbert, Ann. "Single Parent Families: Children as Parents." *Current*, December 1984.

Hunt, Gaillard, ed. *The Writings of James Madison*. New York: G. P. Putnam's Sons, 1906.

Ihlanfeldt, Keith R. *Job Accessibility and the Employment and School Enrollment of Teenagers*. Kalamazoo, Mich.: W. E. Upjohn Institute for Employment Research, 1992.

Ingrassia, Paul, and Joseph B. White. *Comeback: The Fall and Rise of the American Automobile Industry*. New York: Simon and Schuster, 1994.

Jargowsky, P. A. "Ghetto Poverty Among Blacks in the 1980s." *Journal of Policy Analysis and Management*, vol. 13, no. 2 (1994).

Jefferson, Thomas. "First Inaugural Address," March 4, 1801. In vol. 1 of *A Compilation of Messages and Papers of the Presidents*. New York Bureau of National Literature, 1897.

Jencks, Christopher. *Rethinking Social Policy: Race, Poverty, and the Underclass*. New York: HarperCollins, 1992.

———, et al. *Inequality: A Reassessment of the Effect of Family and Schooling in America*. New York: Basic Books, 1972.

———, and Kathryn Edin. "The Real Welfare Problem." *The American Prospect*, no. 1 (Spring 1990).

Jenkins, Kent J. "For Ollie North, Crime Pays." *Washington Post National Weekly Edition*, October 18–24, 1993.

Johnson, Bryan T., and Thomas P. Sheehy. *The Index of Economic Freedom.* Washington, D.C.: Heritage Foundation, 1995.

Jones, E. "Ways in Which Childbearing Affects Women's Employment: Evidence from the National Fertility Study." *Population Studies*, vol. 36, no. 1 (1982).

Karoly, Lynn A., and Gary Burtless. "Demographic Changes, Rising Earnings, Inequality and the Distribution of Personal Well-being." *Demography*, vol. 32, no. 3 (August 1995).

Karst, Kenneth L. *Belonging to America: Equal Citizenship and the Constitution.* New Haven, Conn.: Yale University Press, 1989.

Katz, Michael B. *The Undeserving Poor: From the War on Poverty to the War on Welfare.* New York: Pantheon Books, 1989.

Kelly, Michael. "The Man of the Minute." *The New Yorker*, July 17, 1995.

Kennan, John. "The Elusive Effects of Minimum Wages." *Journal of Economic Literature*, vol. 30, no. 4 (December 1995).

Kinsley, Michael. "The Intellectual Free Lunch: Everybody's Entitled to an Opinion, Right? Wrong." *The New Yorker*, February 6, 1995.

Krugman, Paul. *Peddling Prosperity: Economic Sense and Nonsense in the Age of Diminished Expectations.* New York: W. W. Norton, 1994.

Kuttner, Robert. *The End of Laissez-Faire.* New York: Alfred A. Knopf, 1991.

Lafer, Gordon. "Measuring the Jobs Gap: Labor Demand and the Politics of Federal Employment Policy." Yale University, mimeo, August 1994.

———. "Minority Unemployment: Labor Market Segmentation and the Failure of Job-Training Policy in New York City." *Urban Affairs Quarterly*, vol. 28, no. 2 (December 1992).

Lane, Robert E. *The Market Experience.* Cambridge: Cambridge University Press, 1991.

Levine, David I. *Reinventing the Workplace: How Business and Employees Can Both Win.* Washington, D.C.: Brookings Institution, 1995.

———, and Laura D'Andrea Tyson. "Participation, Productivity, and the Firm's Environment." In Alan Blinder, ed., *Paying for Productivity*, Washington, D.C.: Brookings Institution, 1990.

Lipset, Seymour Martin. *American Exceptionalism: A Double-Edged Sword.* New York: W. W. Norton, 1996.

Locke, John. *An Essay Concerning Human Understanding and a Treatise on the Conduct of the Understanding.* Philadelphia: Hayes and Zell, 1854.

Louv, Richard. "Hope in Hell's Classroom." *New York Times Magazine,* November 25, 1990.

Luker, Kristin. "Dubious Conceptions: The Controversy over Teen Pregnancy." *The American Prospect,* vol. 5 (Spring 1991).

Mack, Joanna, and Stewart Lansley. *Poor Britain.* London: George Allen and Unwin, 1985.

MacLeod, Jay. *Ain't No Makin It: Aspirations and Attainment in a Low-Income Neighborhood.* Boulder, Colo.: Westview Press, 1995.

Males, Mike. "Poverty, Rape, Adult/Teen Sex: Why Pregnancy Prevention Programs Don't Work." *Phi Delta Kappan,* January 1994.

Manley, John F. "American Liberalism and the Democratic Dream: Transcending the American Dream." *Policy Studies Review,* vol. 10, no. 1 (Fall 1990).

Mathias, Peter. *The First Industrial Nation: An Economic History of Britain, 1700–1914.* 2nd ed. London: Routledge, 1983.

McClelland, Peter D. *The American Search for Economic Justice.* Cambridge, Mass.: Basil Blackwell, 1990.

McCoy, Drew R. *The Elusive Republic: Political Economy in Jeffersonian America.* New York: W. W. Norton, 1980.

McCrate, Elaine. "Labor Market Segmentation and Relative Black/White Teenage Birth Rates." *Review of Black Political Economy,* vol. 18 (Spring 1990).

McKerman, John R. *Making the Grade.* Boston: Little, Brown, 1994.

McLanahan, Sara S. "The Consequences of Single Motherhood." *The American Prospect,* no. 18 (Summer 1994).

Mead, Lawrence M. *The New Politics of Poverty: The Nonworking Poor in America.* New York: Basic Books, 1992.

Mishell, Lawrence, and David M. Frankel. *The State of Working America, 1990–91.* Armonk, N.Y.: M. E. Sharpe, 1991.

Moon, J. Donald. *Constructing Community: Moral Pluralism and Tragic Conflicts.* Princeton, N.J.: Princeton University Press, 1993.

Morin, Richard. "The Devil Is in the Details." *Washington Post National Weekly Edition,* January 30–February 5, 1995.

Murray, Charles. "Does Welfare Bring More Babies?" *The American Enterprise*, vol. 5, no. 1 (January/February 1994).

————. *Losing Ground: American Social Policy, 1950–1980*. New York: Basic Books, 1984.

————. "Welfare and the Family: The U.S. Experience." *Journal of Labor Economics*, vol. 2, no. 1 (1993).

National Research Council. *Measuring Poverty: A New Approach*. Washington, D.C.: National Academy Press, 1995.

Nedelsky, Jennifer. *Private Property and the Limits of American Constitutionalism: The Madisonian Framework and Its Legacy*. Chicago: University of Chicago Press, 1990.

Nelson, Richard R. *High-Technology Policies: A Five-Nation Comparison*. Washington, D.C.: American Enterprise Institute, 1984.

Newman, Katherine, and Chauncy Lennon. "The Job Ghetto." *The American Prospect*, no. 122 (Summer 1995).

Nordheimer, Jon. "Welfare-to-Work Plans Show Success Is Difficult to Achieve." *New York Times*, September 1, 1996.

Nozick, Robert. *Anarchy, State, and Utopia*. New York: Basic Books, 1974.

Office of the Federal Register. *U.S. Weekly Compilation of Presidential Documents*. Vol. 18. September–December 1982.

Offner, Paul. "How Workfare Can Work." *The New Republic*, March 14, 1994.

Orshansky, Mollie. "Counting the Poor: Another Look at the Poverty Profile." *Social Security Bulletin*, vol. 28 (January 1965).

Olsen, Randall J., and George Farkas. "The Effect of Economic Opportunity and Family Background on Adolescent Cohabitation and Childbearing Among Low-Income Blacks." *Journal of Labor Economics*, vol. 8, no. 3 (1990).

Padover, Saul K., ed. *The Complete Madison: His Basic Writings*. New York: Harper and Brothers, 1973.

Perloff, Jeffrey M., and Michael L. Wachter. "The New Jobs Tax Credit: An Evaluation of the 1977–1978 Wage Subsidy Program." *American Economic Review*, vol. 69 (May 1979).

Peterson, George E., and Wayne Vroman. "Urban Labor Markets and Economic Opportunity." In George E. Peterson and Wayne Vroman, eds., *Urban Labor Markets and Job Opportunity*. Washington, D.C.: Urban Institute Press, 1992.

Phillips, Leslie. "A Family's Tale." *USA Today*, January 3, 1995.

Piven, Frances F., and Richard A. Cloward. *The New Class War*. New York: Pantheon Books, 1982.

Plotnick, Robert D. "The Effect of Social Policies on Teenage Pregnancy and Childbearing." *Families in Society*, vol. 74, no. 6 (June 1993).

———, and S. Lundberg. "Adolescent Premarital Childbearing." Discussion paper no. 926–90. Institute for Research on Poverty (Madison, Wis.).

Porter, Kirk Harold. *National Party Platforms, 1840–1968*. Urbana, Ill.: University of Illinois Press, 1970.

Raspberry, William. "Blather on Both Sides." *Washington Post National Weekly Edition*, May 6–12, 1996.

Rawls, John. *A Theory of Justice*. Cambridge, Mass.: Harvard University Press, 1971.

Reagan Program for Economic Recovery. "Program for Economic Recovery, White House Report, February 19, 1981." *U.S. Weekly Compilation of Presidential Documents*, vol. 17 (1981).

Reagan, Ronald. "Inaugural Address." In Ellis Sandoz and Cecil V. Crabb, Jr., eds., *A Tide of Discontent*. Washington, D.C.: Congressional Quarterly Press, 1981.

Rector, Robert, et al. "Dispelling the Myth of Income Inequality." *Backgrounder*, June 6, 1989.

Rogers, Jeff, and Wolfgang Steek. "Workplace Representation Overseas: The Works Councils Story." In Richard B. Freeman, ed., *Working Under Different Rules*. New York: Russell Sage Foundation, 1993.

Rothenberg, Winifred Barr. *From Market-Places to a Market Economy: The Transformation of Rural Massachusetts, 1750–1850*. Chicago: University of Chicago Press, 1993.

Rothstein, Richard. "The Global Hiring Hall." *The American Prospect*, no. 17 (Spring 1994).

Royster, Charles. *A Revolutionary People at War: The Continental Army and American Character, 1775–1783*. Chapel Hill, N.C.: University of North Carolina Press, 1979.

Ruccio, Kenneth P. "Pork and the Public Interest." *The American Prospect*, no. 17 (Spring 1994).

Ruggles, Patricia. *Drawing the Line: Alternative Poverty Measures and Their Implications for Public Policy*. Washington, D.C.: Urban Institute Press, 1990.

Rustin, Bayard. "From Protest to Politics: The Civil Rights Movement." *Commentary*, vol. 39, no. 2 (February 1965).

———. "Civil Rights." *Commentary*, vol. 39, no. 6 (June 1965).

Samuelson, Robert J. "End Affirmative Action." *Washington Post National Weekly Edition*, March 6–12, 1995.

Sandel, Michael J. *Democracy's Discontent: America in Search of a Public Philosophy*. Cambridge, Mass.: Belknap Press of Harvard University Press, 1996.

Schiller, Bradley R. *The Economics of Poverty and Discrimination*. Englewood Cliffs, N.J.: Prentice-Hall, 1980.

Schlebecker, John T. *Whereby We Thrive: A History of American Farming, 1607–1972*. Ames, Iowa: Iowa State University Press, 1975.

Schor, Juliet B. *The Overworked American*. New York: Basic Books, 1991.

Schorr, Daniel. "Washington Notebook." *The New Leader*, March 13–27, 1995.

Schwarz, John E. *America's Hidden Success: A Reassessment of Public Policy from Kennedy to Reagan*. New York: W. W. Norton, 1987.

———, and Thomas J. Volgy. "Experiments in Employment—A British Cure." *Harvard Business Review*, vol. 66, no. 2 (March–April 1988).

———, and Thomas J. Volgy. *The Forgotten Americans: Thirty Million Working Poor in the Land of Opportunity*. New York: W. W. Norton, 1992.

Seltzer, Judith A., and Daniel R. Meyer. "Child Support and Children's Well-being." *Focus*, vol. 17, no. 3 (Spring 1996).

Shapiro, Matthew D. "Comments and Discussion." *Brookings Papers on Economic Activity*, vol. 1 (1994). Washington, D.C.: Brookings Institution, 1994.

Shklar, Judith N. *American Citizenship: The Quest for Inclusion*. Cambridge, Mass.: Harvard University Press, 1991.

Shogren, Elizabeth. "Discord Among GOP Senators Threatens to Stall Welfare Bill." *Los Angeles Times*, June 16, 1995.

Shuman, R Baird. "Big Guns, Thwarted Dreams: School Violence and the English Teacher." *English Journal*, vol. 84, no. 5 (September 1995).

Sinopoli, Richard C. *The Foundations of American Citizenship*. New York: Oxford University Press, 1992.

Skocpol, Theda. *Social Policy in the United States: Future Possibilities in Historical Perspective*. Princeton, N.J.: Princeton University Press, 1995.

———. *Protecting Soldiers and Mothers: The Political Origins of Social Policy in the United States.* Cambridge, Mass.: Harvard University Press, 1992.

Skogan, Wesley G. *Disorder and Decline: Crime and the Spiral of Decay in American Neighborhoods.* New York: Free Press, 1990.

Smeeding, Timothy M., et al. *Poverty, Inequality, and Income Distribution in Comparative Perspective.* New York: Harvester Wheatsheaf, 1990.

Smith, Adam. *Inquiry into the Nature and Causes of the Wealth of Nations.* London: Methuen, 1930.

Smith, Vern E., et al. "Children of the Underclass." *Newsweek,* September 11, 1989.

Streenivasan, Gopal. *The Limits of Lockean Rights in Property.* New York: Oxford University Press, 1995.

Tomlins, Christopher L. *Law, Labor, and Ideology in the Early American Republic.* New York: Cambridge University Press, 1993.

Tocqueville, Alexis de. *Democracy in America* Vol. 1. New York: Vintage Books, 1945.

Trillin, Calvin. "Drawing the Line." *The New Yorker,* December 12, 1994.

"The Trouble with Success." *The Economist,* March 12, 1994.

Uchitelle, Louis. "From Government Cash to a New Living Wage." *Beacon Journal,* April 9, 1996.

———. "The Humbling of the Harvard Man." *New York Times,* March 6, 1994.

Upchurch, D. M., and J. McCarthy. "The Timing of a First Birth and High School Completion." *American Sociological Review,* vol. 55 (1990).

Vickers, Daniel. "Competency and Competition: Economic Culture in Early America." *William and Mary Quarterly,* January 1990.

Viscusi, W. Kip. "Market Incentives for Criminal Behavior." In Richard B. Freeman and Harry J. Holzer, eds., *The Black Youth Employment Crisis.* Chicago: University of Chicago Press, 1986.

Vobejda, Barbara. "Training for Work from Welfare." *Washington Post National Weekly Edition,* July 7–13, 1995.

Volgy, Thomas J., John E. Schwarz, and Lawrence Imwalle. "In Search of Economic Well-being: The Relation Between Worker Power and Economic Returns in Ten Industrial Nations." *American Journal of Political Science,* vol. 40, no. 4 (November 1996).

Walzer, Michael. *Spheres of Justice: A Defense of Pluralism and Equality.* New York: Basic Books, 1983.

Weidenbaum, Murray L. "The Costs of Government Regulation of Business." Joint Economic Committee, U.S. Congress, April 10, 1978.

———. *The Future of Government Regulation*. New York: Amacom, 1979.

Welch, Finis. "Black-White Differences in Returns to Schooling." *American Economic Review*, vol. 63 (December 1973).

Whitehead, Barbara Dafoe. "Dan Quayle Was Right." *Atlantic Monthly*, April 1993.

Whitman, David. "The Myth of Reform." *U.S. News & World Report*, January 16, 1995.

Will, George. "Two Years Later." *Washington Post*, January 19, 1995.

Williams, Walter. "The Result of Welfare in Modern-Day Slavery." *Post and Courier* (Charleston, S.C.), November 22, 1995.

Wills, Garry. *Lincoln at Gettysburg: The Words That Remade America*. New York: Simon and Schuster, 1992.

Wilson, Alan B., Travis Hirschi, and Glen Elder. "Richmond Youth Project: Secondary School Study, Technical Report #1." Survey Research Center, University of California, Berkley mimeo, 1965.

Wilson, William Julius. *The Truly Disadvantaged: The Inner City, the Underclass, and Public Policy*. Chicago: University of Chicago Press, 1987.

INDEX